"What better way to crea⬚⬚⬚⬚⬚⬚⬚⬚⬚⬚⬚⬚⬚⬚⬚⬚⬚⬚⬚⬚⬚⬚⬚⬚⬚⬚⬚⬚⬚⬚s with our daughters than ⬚⬚⬚⬚⬚⬚⬚⬚⬚⬚⬚⬚⬚⬚⬚⬚⬚⬚⬚⬚⬚⬚⬚⬚⬚⬚⬚n, with the evidence of his lo⬚⬚⬚⬚⬚⬚⬚⬚⬚⬚⬚⬚⬚⬚⬚⬚⬚ ⬚⬚⬚ concept behind this book is brilliant in its simplicity. Trish Donohue's discussion guides, with their wisdom and transparency, are exactly what women need to make these conversations happen. This will not be a book that sits on your shelf. It will be a well-worn and beloved treasure between you and the young women in your life, be it a daughter, niece, granddaughter, or friend."

Debra Bell, Author; speaker; educator

"Every mom longs to have a close and enduring friendship with her daughter. In *Between Us Girls*, author and mom Trish Donohue takes a busy mom by one hand and her young daughter by the other, and leads them together into a deep understanding of God's Word and a sweet experience of fellowship with one another. Short chapters and engaging questions make this a book that daughters will be eager to read and talk about with their moms. As a mother and daughter who have a very close friendship, we are excited to recommend and use this book to pass on a legacy of biblical womanhood to the next generation."

Carolyn Mahaney and Nicole Mahaney Whitacre, Coauthors of *Girl Talk*, *Feminine Appeal*, and *True Beauty*

"Have you ever wondered exactly how to have meaningful conversations with your daughter? If so, this is the book for you. Trish Donohue helps moms build a deep relationship with their daughters with good questions that encourage openness and honesty. Through it all, she weaves the story of Jesus and how it relates to all aspects of life: peer pressure, friendships, appearance, church, siblings, fears, clothes, and much more. Let Trish take you on a walk with your daughter, enjoying the world that God has created, and sharing how to walk in it with faith and confidence in what Jesus has done."

Rose Marie Miller, Author of *From Fear to Freedom* and *Nothing Is Impossible with God*; coauthor of *The Gospel-Centered Parent*

"In the midst of our busy lives, it is easy to forsake our best intentions for purposeful parenting. Adding to the struggle, is not knowing how to enter in to the world of our girls with gospel truth. *Between Us Girls* provides a deliberate plan for bonding together over God's Word in a way that is fun, without sacrificing depth. What I love most though is Trish Donohue's ability to hand our daughters the biblical lenses to see each topic and the world around them rightly."

Kristen Hatton, Author of *Get Your Story Straight: A Teen's Guide to Learning & Living the Gospel*

"As a father of three grown daughters I have listened to a lot of mother-daughter conversations over the years. Talk about going deep real quick. But deep can be confusing, even misguided at times. That's what I love about this book! Trish provides a winsome path toward conversations that can be deep and wise—full of good fruit for both moms and daughters because they are truth-guided and grace-focused. Who couldn't use that kind of help?"

Andy Farmer, Pastor; author of *Real Peace* and *Trapped*

"As a mother of a twelve-year-old girl, I am always looking for relatable ways to share my love for the gospel with my daughter. *Between Us Girls* does just that. Trish Donohue has set up a helpful, easy, and fun rhythm for discussions between mothers and daughters. You will enjoy the journey of getting to know your daughter and opening your life to her as you share about fears, faith, likes, and life."

Jessica Thompson, Author/Speaker

"*Between Us Girls* is a mother-daughter discipleship guide covering many topics essential to life and godliness. For each topic, the guide demonstrates God's intention, sin's hindrance, the gospel's solution, and a practical application. Pertinent Scripture passages, sound and creative doctrinal teaching, and inviting discussion starters fill its pages. The guide is concise, simple, and enjoyable to use. *Between Us Girls* is a great idea. I heartily recommend it for Christian moms and daughters everywhere."

Starr Meade, Author of *Training Hearts, Teaching Minds*

"*Between Us Girls* by Trish Donohue is the resource moms have been looking for to help them connect with their growing daughters. Trish weaves together meaningful Bible study, helpful questions, and life applications in a way that is provoking but not preachy. My wife is excited to start using it in our home."

Marty Machowski, Family pastor; author of *The Ology* and *The Gospel Story for Kids* books and curriculum

BETWEEN
US
GIRLS

Walks and Talks for Moms and Daughters

Trish Donohue

New
Growth
Press

WWW.NEWGROWTHPRESS.COM

New Growth Press, Greensboro, NC 27404

Cover/Interior Design: Trish Mahoney
Typesetting and E-book: Lisa Parnell

ISBN: 978-1-942572-77-0 (Print)
ISBN: 978-1-942572-78-7 (eBook)

Library of Congress Cataloging-in-Publication Data
    Names: Donohue, Trish, 1970- author.
    Title: Between us girls : walks and talks for moms and daughters / Trish
        Donohue.
    Description: Greensboro, NC : New Growth Press, 2016. | Includes
        bibliographical references and index.
    Identifiers: LCCN 2015042361| ISBN 9781942572770 (print) | ISBN
9781942572787
        (ebook)
    Subjects: LCSH: Mothers and daughters--Religious aspects--Christianity.
    Classification: LCC BV4529.18 .D65 2016 | DDC 248.8/431--dc23
    LC record available at http://lccn.loc.gov/2015042361

Printed in China

23 22 21 20 19 18 17 16   1 2 3 4 5

For Bryn and Shannon.
May our walks continue,
and may the hill always be in view.

Contents

Acknowledgments

I am grateful to Marty Machowski who encouraged me to consider this project and to the team at New Growth Press for all their help. Barbara Juliani, Nancy Winter, Cheryl White, Gretchen Logterman, thank you for making this happen, and thank you to Trish Mahoney who designed the cover.

Thanks to the many friends who offered suggestions, including Rachel Hayes who also reviewed the draft.

Thank you to my mom, Naomi, for teaching me about Jesus at a young age, and to Covenant Fellowship Church for enlarging my vision of all that he is.

Adam, Asher, Bryn, and Shannon, thanks for making mother-hood a joy and for your encouragement and patience as I worked on this. I am ready to close the laptop!

Jim, I couldn't have done this without you. I'm so grateful for your love and support, your careful review and edits, and your help in applying the gospel, which you love more than anyone I know.

A Word to Moms

....

If you're flipping through this book, you probably have a daughter, and I can make a few educated guesses about you:

- **You love her very much.**
- **You feel like she is growing up way too fast.**
- **You would like to spend more time with her in meaningful conversation.**
- **You are sometimes overwhelmed by all there is to talk about.**

Me too. I have two daughters and although we have lots of spontaneous conversations, I'm not always sure we're hitting the most important topics. Sometimes I wish I had a cheat sheet.

That's what this book is meant to be: a cheat sheet. It is a compilation of twenty-six biblically based talks you can have with your daughter on significant topics. If you meet weekly, you'll be done in six months; if you meet biweekly, you'll finish in a year. If it ends up taking you five years, that's fine too.

In each of your times together, you and your daughter will be studying God's Word, asking one another questions about your thoughts and experiences, and building real fellowship into your relationship. No prep time is needed, so all you need to do is schedule a time, grab this book and a Bible, and head to your destination of choice, whether it's a coffee shop or your comfiest couch.

You'll find that the book addresses both of you (so that you can model openness and honesty for your daughter), but the content is written with her in mind. Reading each chapter aloud to her will work best, making sure you stop to look up the Scriptures and answer the questions—both of which are essential in getting the most out of your times together. If you use this book with multiple daughters or even their friends, feel free to tweak the questions to meet them where they are.

The topics covered are not exhaustive; they couldn't be. There are just too many things moms and daughters need to talk about. Neither do they plumb the depths of wisdom on every subject. But they will get you started, springboarding you into further conversations that could fill volumes. Although the talks can stand alone, I've learned that any injection of fun can up the level of anticipation. So if you add a special snack, drink, or meeting place to the repertoire, it will help the cause!

You'll notice an appendix entitled, "Our Protection" in the back of the book. This deals with the sensitive but important topic of sexual abuse. It's separate from the other talks because it has a slightly different format and because it relates to several of the other chapters—not because it is less significant. Please use this tool after whatever chapter you decide is best, but don't miss the opportunity to have this vital conversation.

Enjoy these sweet times, moms, and remember that you are God's perfect choice to love and train your daughter. And she is God's perfect choice for you.

Sincerely,
Trish

P.S. If you plan to go through this book with a girl who is not your daughter, I applaud you! Whether you are an aunt, a family friend, or a mentor, we need more women like you. Thank you for reaching out and investing in the girls God has placed in your life. By simply changing the mother/daughter language as you read, this book should be easy to use in both one-on-one and small group contexts.

Walk 1
Our Conversations

Imagine strolling along a country road on a cool evening. The orange sun is at your back and a little brook zigzags along beside you, splashing over rocks and sticks. Stooping to pick a few buttercups, you place them carefully behind your ear and head toward home wearing a contented smile.

Now imagine you're on the same country road, but it's noon. You can smell the manure freshly spread on the field nearby, and the flies are buzzing so loudly you can't hear any other noise. It's hot. Really hot. You lick your lips, remembering the water bottle you left in the fridge at home. "I hate this road," you grumble as you kick a stone and stub your toe.

Every walk is so different from the next, isn't it? Some are enchanting, some are miserable, and most are somewhere in between. In Deuteronomy, parents are instructed to teach their children God's truth whatever kind of walk they are on. And that's not all. They're to teach their children when they relax at home, when they go to bed, and when they roll out of bed in the morning. That's a lot of teaching!

God's truth is the most important topic we could ever talk about, but sometimes it seems a little boring. Sometimes neither you, nor your mom, really know what to say. So I'd like to welcome you to our first official stroll. We're going to explore quite a bit of territory together. We'll cross meadows and pant our way up hills, but we'll find beauty along the way each time. We'll explore God's call on our lives, and the two of you will get to know each other even better in the process.

Before we go any further, take a minute to look at each other. Go ahead; stare right into each other's eyes. Are they brown, or black, or blue, or green? Or purple? Do you know that person in there? Whether she looks exactly like you or completely different, she is God's perfect choice for you. And since he is infinitely wise, you *know* he chose well. So let's start talking.

MOMS: What are two things you adore about your daughter?

GIRLS: What is one thing you love about your mom?

BOTH: If you could have any eye color in the world, what would you choose?

The world around us sometimes misses the gift a mother-daughter relationship can be. If you watch much TV, you'll see that moms are often portrayed as clueless and daughters as disrespectful. Girls on those shows usually share their feelings with friends and hide their feelings from their moms. But they are missing out on one of the best presents God has given us. God's designs are always best, and if he wanted you to learn the important truths of life from your friend across the street, he would have said so. But God tells moms (and dads) to do this job.

Read Deuteronomy 11:18–19, the passage we talked about earlier, to figure out what the job looks like.

The reason for so much talking is that there is so much to talk about.

> **BOTH:** As quickly as you can, list ten topics that moms and daughters could have good conversations about. Go!

Those ten were just the tip of the iceberg. There are hundreds more. But we don't just want to hear our own voices; we want to hear God share his perspective on these topics. After all, he designed us. So make sure you always bring a Bible on our walks. We'll get hopelessly lost without it.

Turn to Isaiah 40:8 and read what it says about the Bible.

We'll be traipsing through a lot of flowerbeds and weed patches during these walks. Eventually, every budding flower wilts, and every bullying weed shrivels up, but not the Word of God. It will never fade or weaken or die. God's truth stands forever, and on it we want to base our conversations.

Now let's map out the plan. The two of you, grab a snack and find a private place. It could be the kitchen table, a hammock, or a hot air balloon, as long as you're undistracted. That's when the walk begins. You won't physically be walking (unless you want to), but you'll be "walking" through a particular topic, talking to each other, listening to what God has to say, and asking each other questions.

During each walk, we'll go through four areas:

1. THE GARDEN. Our garden section describes God's vision for us. This reminds us of the Garden of Eden—a perfect place for God's perfect plan for Adam and Eve. A place unspoiled by sin.

> **GIRLS:** If you could grow one thing in a garden, what would it be?

2. THE WEEDS. In this section, we'll talk about how sin messes everything up. That's what happened when Adam and Eve chose to turn away from God's design and follow their own. The daisies wilted, and thorns and weeds sprang up.

> **GIRLS:** Why do you think people hate pulling weeds?

3. THE HILL. The hill we'll be passing is the hill of Calvary. It represents the gospel: the good news of Jesus's death and resurrection. On this hill we'll see the cross where Jesus died to rescue us from the grip of sin and where he gives us power to follow him. Risen to life, he tends our weedy gardens and makes them beautiful again.

> **GIRLS:** What is the highest hill you have ever climbed?

4. THE FIELD. We'll end our walk in the field. This is where we take the truths we've learned and go to work. Seeds are planted and fruit grows—we watch the gospel change everything. In the field, we'll talk about ways to apply what we've learned to our everyday lives.

GIRLS: If you had to skip, sprint, or cartwheel across a field, which would you choose?

MOMS: What are some topics you wish you would have discussed with your mom when you were young?

GIRLS: What are you most looking forward to in these times? Are there any topics you hope we talk about?

BOTH: Take turns guessing one another's favorite snack (and girls, don't forget to remind your mom you'll need one for these walks!).

Walk 2
Our Foundation

Today we're going to take our most important walk together, so I hope you're well rested and have a granola bar in your pocket. In fact, I'll go so far as to say this is the most important walk anyone could ever take. More important than a bride's march down the aisle, or a president's steps to the White House, or a climber's trek up Mount Everest. And because this is the best walk with the best view, pay close attention. We don't want to miss anything.

THE GARDEN. We'll pick up the trail in a wild and wonderful garden, where a man and a woman waded in streams and picked berries, and spent time with someone who amazed and delighted them—their Maker, who filled their hearts with joy.

Then Satan, disguised as a snake, came and told them a lie. He told them God's ways were not best for them and that maybe God's laws were even a little selfish. Maybe God didn't really mean the things he said. Maybe God wasn't good. They listened to the snake; after all, they should be able to think for themselves, shouldn't they?

So the man and woman believed the lie about God and chose to disobey their great and loving Creator. They brought sin, like a poisonous fog, into their heaven on earth—and the flowers turned to weeds.

GIRLS: If you were Eve living in Eden, what animal would you like to walk up to and pet?

MOMS: Have you ever listened to lies about God or had trouble believing his ways are good?

THE WEEDS. The weeds spread like a disease and spoiled the garden; and sin spread, and spoiled hearts. Instead of pleasing God, people pleased themselves. Instead of loving others, people loved themselves. They rolled their eyes at God's laws. They started believing that God was just a nice guy who had made a nice garden. They forgot that as well as being kind and loving, God was holy and dazzling, and even a little scary—the way a great king or queen is.

The truth was that God was holy and righteous whether they believed it or not. Like any good ruler, he had to punish crime. He had to deal with sin.

Let's take a break to check the trail map here. We want to make sure we're going in the right direction.

Read Romans 3:23.

That "all" includes moms, daughters—everybody. Although it's hard to think about, let's see what the punishment for our rebellion against God is.

Read 2 Thessalonians 1:9.

That's not fun to read. It seems like we were just walking through a sunshiny garden. Now all this darkness and tangled weeds . . .

God, somehow, still loved us even though we rejected him and disobeyed his rule. He sent all kinds of messengers—prophets—to remind us of his laws and his love, but nobody listened for long. Then he sent someone else.

THE HILL. Jesus should have come in a dazzling display of power, riding on a lightning bolt or something, but God put his Son in a smelly stable, and he grew up to save the smelliest of sinners. Even though he was tempted just like we are, Jesus lived every day without committing even one tiny sin. One lie would have wrecked God's whole plan, which was to give his people a way out.

> **GIRLS:** In what area do you think it was most difficult for Jesus to resist sin? Doing chores? Getting along with his siblings? School?

Jesus really did live a sinless life. The religious leaders didn't like that he claimed to be God, so they turned everyone against him, and Jesus allowed them to lead him up a hill called Calvary and nail his hands and feet to a cross. He let them lift him up so that he would suffer and die in front of everyone. He took our place, bearing the punishment we deserved for sin. He switched places with us. He was punished so we wouldn't be. He took our weedy, sin-soiled life, and gave us his perfect one.

Read 2 Corinthians 5:21.

That's quite a mouthful, but do you see the switch? We were the sinful ones and Jesus was the righteous one, but he switched. He became sin so we could become righteous and clean. Jesus lifts our burden of sin and dresses us in his own righteousness. The Bible says that if we repent of our sins and believe that Jesus died for us (Mark 1:15), we'll be forgiven and become a child of God—a child of the King. It's like walking into a shining castle filled with gifts and blessings to explore. We'll discover many of them as we walk and talk our way through this book.

Are you beginning to see why this walk is so important? It's because we're walking through God's rescue plan for us. We've seen a holy King who loves his people. We've seen the wreckage of sin. We've seen God's rescue mission through Jesus. We've looked at the only hope we have for forgiveness, joy, and freedom—and living forever in heaven.

Without understanding this plan, the rest of this book will sound like this: "Be a better person, blah blah blah; make sure you are a good girl, blah blah; don't be like those bad girls, blah blah blah." A message like that is a pile of fool's gold: worthless. Although we are loved by God and created to bring him glory, every one of us has made a mess of things and needs Jesus to fix it. When we are forgiven and washed clean, then we can begin to grow to be like Christ. We can grow to become the people he designed us to be; not so we become proud and important, but so we reflect God's love, kindness, and beauty—and bring glory to him.

Now that we've leveled off and the field is in sight, let's talk a little more.

GIRLS: Adam and Eve were probably terrified when they realized they had sinned against God. Have you ever felt bothered or scared by your sinfulness?

MOMS: Describe how you realized your need for a Savior. Was it a sudden or gradual? What details do you remember?

GIRLS: Have you repented of your sin and received Jesus's gift of righteousness? If not, have you ever thought about it?

THE FIELD

- Why do you think this walk is more important than the others? Why would skipping it make all the others meaningless?

- Two of the treasures we find in the castle of the gospel are forgiveness of sins and adoption into God's family. See if you can list three more.

- Take turns telling each other Jesus's good news, as well as you can, in less than thirty seconds.

- Read about Jesus's crucifixion and resurrection together sometime this week; then take a few minutes to thank God for his sacrificial love.

Walk 3
Our Words

It's hard not to giggle at someone repeating a tongue twister. Her mouth contorts, and her words clog up like cars in a traffic jam. Let's try one: "toy boat, toy boat, toy boat, toy boat, toy boat." Go ahead, say it. Now say it faster. Now try, "rubber baby buggy bumpers," or "freshly-fried flying fish." Are your lips turning inside out? Words are just groups of letters, but when we put them together in a certain order, they do surprising things.

THE GARDEN. Consider all the work our words do each day. We use them to encourage, ask for help, sing, complain, tell stories, relay facts, read aloud, lie, express joy, snap at our siblings, whisper "I love you," and maybe even sneeze if we actually yell, "Atchoo!" Words are an enormous part of our lives.

In middle school science class, I remember a friend informing me that my purple eyeshadow looked ridiculous. Why can I still recall those words? Why can I still remember my mom, each night as she tucked me in, saying, "Good night, I love you, sweet dreams"? The reason is that words are powerful. They can sting or soothe, hurt or heal, and God wants us to use their remarkable power for good.

MOMS: What specific words do you remember from a moment in your childhood? Why do you think you remember them?

GIRLS: What are happy words you remember being said to you? Are there any unhappy words that have stuck in your memory?

Sometimes we shrug off the importance of our words. "They're not that big of a deal," we tell ourselves. But God's Word disagrees.

Read Ephesians 4:29.

That's a pretty tall order. When God gave us the gift of words, he had big plans for them. He wanted them to be used to strengthen, support, build up, and spread grace wherever they went, like a flower girl spreads rose petals before the bride.

Speaking of sweetness, **read Proverbs 16:24**.

GIRLS: Describe the sweetest concoction you think you could create. Use no more than five ingredients and make it yummy.

In the days this verse was written, a honeycomb would have been the most sugary food imaginable. Think cotton candy, ice cream, and Pixy Stix, but maybe not all piled together. Did you know we can actually bring sweetness to those around us using our words?

Encouragement is a good example of this. Girls, when you think you've written a horrible paper and your teacher scrawls, "Excellent job!" on your paper, that's a mouthful of chocolate ice cream to your soul. When you're sick of emptying the dishwasher, and your mom tells you how much she appreciates your faithfulness and hard work, she's feeding your heart cotton candy, and the job is a little easier. We all feel weak and discouraged sometimes, and that's why God wants us to use our words to encourage each other. In fact, let's practice.

GIRLS: What is one thing you've seen your mom do really well this week?

MOMS: Where have you seen your daughter grow in the past year?

Our words can be sweet in other ways too. We can pray for a hurting friend, thank someone for how he serves us, or answer a sharp comment with gentleness. We can use our cheerful voice to set a tone of joy wherever we are. Remember, words are more powerful than we think.

THE WEEDS. I have to admit, sometimes my voice is not a honeycomb. Sometimes it's an old, sour lemon slice with mold growing on it.

MOMS: What rough words do you find yourself saying? Ask your daughter if you need some help.

GIRLS: When we have the opportunity to be sweet, why do we often use our words to discourage, complain, or tear down?

To find the answer, **read Luke 6:45**.

Whatever is in our hearts spills out into our words. If a well is full of clean spring water, it will bring refreshment. If it's full of muck, well, you can guess the result. Our hearts work the same way. What's inside comes out. If our hearts are full of kindness and trust in God, then our words will reveal that. If they're full of self-pity and jealousy, people around us will be splashed with the "muck" of our words.

Because sin has polluted our hearts, selfishness, anger, and ungratefulness bubble up far too often. Is there any hope for us to be the sweet communicators God wants us to be?

THE HILL. God tells his people in Ezekiel 36:26, "I will give you a new heart, and a new spirit I will put within you." When Jesus paid for our sins on the cross, he was also buying us a new heart. When we ask him to forgive us and cleanse us, the power of sin is broken in us. That doesn't mean we won't sin anymore, but it does mean that we are no longer slaves to sin. God's Spirit can give us hearts that overflow with honey.

My girls and I have a code word that we sometimes whisper to each other when our speech needs a little sweetening. It won't be a secret any longer, but I'll tell you anyway: It's the word *honeycomb*. And when I hear that word gently whispered in my ear, I know I need to run to my Savior for help and say, "Lord, sweeten my heart and words." And then I try again because God loves to give us second chances.

Psalm 19:14 gives us a great prayer to pray about our speech: "Let the words of my mouth and the meditation of my heart be acceptable in your sight, O Lord, my rock and my redeemer." That's a prayer we can pray as we get out of bed in the morning, before we even open our mouths to speak.

 THE FIELD

- What secret code word could you use to remind each other to sweeten your words?
- Is there something in your speech that you need to confess to the Lord and ask for help to overcome?
- Who in your family could you surprise with words of encouragement this week? What could you encourage them about?
- Who, outside your family, could you bless with your words this week? Could you invite a lonely girl at school to join you and your friends? Could you write a kind note to an older woman at church who doesn't have family close by? The options are many. Pick one.
- If you have an electronic device or access to social media, what ways can you use it to promote sweet speech? What ways can it tempt you to make bad choices with your words?

Put on your hiking boots, because our walk is going to take us up and down, and up and down, and up and down again. On the top of the hills, we'll feel the wind in our hair and the sun on our face. At the bottom of the valleys, we'll wade through swamps and feel our way in the gloom. There is only one topic that could take us on a journey as crazy as this: our feelings.

🌳 **THE GARDEN.** Believe it or not, God created our feelings and emotions. The Bible tells us that there is a time to laugh and a time to cry, so we know emotions in themselves are good. Can you imagine Adam and Eve plodding around the Garden of Eden stating in bland voices, "This. Piece. Of. Land. Appears. Adequate." No way! They were probably splashing in streams, cracking up over the crazy animals, and oohing and aahing over that first sunset. Their emotions gave glory and praise to the Designer of that incredible place. And you, no doubt, have experienced some big emotions yourself.

> **GIRLS:** Recall a time when you felt so happy you thought you'd burst?
>
> **MOMS:** When were you so nervous it felt like a hundred butterflies were dancing in your stomach?

Feelings are a gift from God. There are sad times when the right thing to do is cry like a baby, and there are happy times when the only appropriate response is to laugh your head off. Our feelings make us human. They make us giddy with joy as we race down the beach and dive into that first wave. They make us grieve when we lose someone who means the world to us. Best of all, they help us long for and love Jesus. But sometimes they're not so easy to deal with.

✳ **THE WEEDS.** Sometimes our feelings blow in like a hurricane and, instead of standing firm, we let them sweep us up. Our thoughts whisper:

- **"Just mope and pout. You didn't get what you wanted, so don't even try to be nice."**
- **"You're going to be embarrassed in gym class tomorrow. You know you won't be able to run the mile fast enough. Imagine how dumb you'll feel."**
- **"There's no way your mom will understand. Just tell her a bit of the truth, not all of it."**
- **"It really stinks that you're not allowed to go to that movie. Your parents are out of it. Slam the door hard so they know you're mad."**

BOTH: Which of these is most familiar to you?

Feelings can be convincing, and they can be loud. They're not wrong in themselves, but they can tempt us to think wrong thoughts. When our feelings tempt us to disobey God, we need to let them know they can't push us around. Then we need to grab the most powerful weapon we can—God's Word—and blast them with the truth. In fact, let's practice fighting the four feelings above.

Read the Scripture passage and answer the questions:

1. 1 Thessalonians 5:16–18: How could this passage be used to combat our feelings of grumpiness?
2. Philippians 4:6–7: How could this knock the sword right out of worry's hand?
3. Proverbs 12:22: How does this verse strike at fear that tempts us to lie?
4. James 1:19: How does this fight the movie-missing madness?

The Bible is crammed with weapons like these verses. As we become more familiar with the words of God, we'll get better at fighting and taming our reactions to our feelings. It will be a whole lot easier if you have some help though, and that's why God has given you each other. God has put someone who knows you very well right in the same house with you. Now we can encourage and pray for each other when those feelings start getting feisty.

MOMS: Describe a time when your feelings tried to boss you around. What truths help you fight against sinful reactions to your feelings?

GIRLS: Is there a feeling that has been hanging around you recently? Maybe you feel left out, or jealous, or scared, or confused about something. Share it with your mom. She's probably had the same feeling.

Not all feelings are clearly right or wrong, and these are some of the hardest to deal with. They waltz in when we're least expecting them. We wake up feeling sad for no reason at all. Maybe a wave of joy surprises us. Some days everything our brother does drives us nuts, and other days we want to hug him. Sometimes life feels hopeless and we just can't shake it, or we're convinced, irrationally, that nobody likes us.

 THE HILL. Girls, even though we have Scripture to wield and our moms to encourage us, we will still find ourselves in the battle with feelings. We may find our hearts overflowing with anger, complaints, embarrassment, or jealousy. We may feel like we're under a gray cloud of gloom that the sun can't evaporate. But if we're Christians, we have a Friend who fights for us and with us. We can run to him for help when we see those tidal waves of feelings coming near. He gives us power to respond well to the emotions that hit us, and he picks us up when we fall. When Jesus died on the cross, he conquered sin and death. So instead of flopping down in defeat when we fail, we can know that even if we lost a particular battle, Jesus has won the war. We can ask for his forgiveness and help, grab the weapon of God's Word, and keep fighting. The good news doesn't depend on what we do, but on what he did. Even in our worst moments, God is now our Father, and he loves us, understands us, comforts us, knows our weaknesses, and cherishes us.

THE FIELD

- Does our culture tell us that we should control our feelings, or that our feelings should control us? (Culture just means the things we see around us like movies and books and music and TV.)
- How can remembering what Jesus did for us help us when we are in a rotten mood?
- As you look at the coming week, is there a particular feeling that you know is coming your way? Look for a weapon of Scripture right now and underline it in your Bible.
- Would memorizing one of the verses we looked at today help the two of you with a common feeling? If so, commit it to memory now.

Walk 5
Our Friendships

Do you remember the tongue twisters we tried a couple walks ago? We found out that words can do funny things to our lips. They can also do funny things to our hearts. Take the word *friendship* for example. It's a pleasant word. But it can leave us floating on air like a puffy cloud or empty and torn like a popped balloon.

We all long for friendship because God designed us to be relational, to give and receive love and enjoy community. Sometimes we have lots of friends, and sometimes we have few. Sometimes we have easy friendships, and sometimes we have difficult ones. Sometimes we can be the difficult friend. Let's wander through the garden and take a closer look at the original design.

THE GARDEN. Even before Adam and Eve were created, a most beautiful friendship existed. Before the stars were lit, before the leaves were stitched together, before the riverbeds were carved, friends enjoyed each other's company. The Father, Son, and Holy Spirit glorified, delighted in, and served each other. They probably laughed together too. When our amazing three-in-one God created humans, he gave us the same gift of friendship. That desire to love and be loved didn't come from us, it came from him.

There is nothing like laughing hysterically with a friend over something ridiculous, feeling comfortable walking into her house, or looking forward to a special time together. But sometimes there are even deeper reasons to love a friend.

MOMS: Who has been a good friend to you? What qualities in friends have you come to appreciate over the years?

GIRLS: Who is a special friend in your life? What about this friend do you most enjoy?

Read John 15:12–13.

To love others the way Christ loved us means putting their needs before our own. Real friendship is about loving others and not worrying so much about yourself. Sin wants to turn those good plans inside out. Sin tempts us to think of ourselves first. That's where a lot of friendships get tangled up in the thorns, and the pricks can really sting.

THE WEEDS. Let's slow down the pace today and embark on a nature study—to be precise, a weed study.

Read Proverbs 27:4.

GIRLS: Why could jealousy be even more damaging than anger and wrath?

Jealousy doesn't seem all that bad. After all, we just want something someone else has. We want to be popular like someone else is; we want to wear cool clothes; or we want to be the soccer star for a change. Maybe we're jealous of others' friendships. "Why does she get invited to everything?" "Why did they get together without telling me?" And slowly, that little struggle with jealousy isn't so little anymore. We begin judging our friends and thinking bitter thoughts about them, and before we know it, that thick nasty weed is choking out the green shoots of friendship.

Read Proverbs 13:20 to find another weed in the friendship garden.

You probably haven't stood in your driveway holding a sign that reads, "Fools Welcome. If you're a fool, I want to be friends with YOU." But sometimes we realize that's what has happened. Our friends are what the Bible calls fools: they don't respect authority, they aren't kind to others, and they are sometimes plain old mean. We become like the people we hang around with, so it's important that we look for "wise" friends, and it's important to be a wise friend ourselves. Our friends won't ever be perfect, and we won't ever be perfect either, but God's words are true: If we walk with the wise, we'll become wise.

MOMS: How have you seen wise and foolish friendships influence you?

GIRLS: Do you have difficult friendships? What makes them difficult?

Some other pesky thorns that threaten friendship are:
- **Gossip: We gossip when we speak unkindly about people behind their backs, or listen to others do the same.**

- **Keeping people out: Others can be hurt when we exclude them from our group of friends by telling secrets or ignoring them.**
- **Laziness: Being a good friend requires effort, and laziness can get in the way.**

THE HILL. I'm glad we don't have to end this walk with a "weed study." The gospel has so much to say to us.

What if you knew that a very special person loved you so much that he would give his life for you? What if you knew that you had a best friend who promised never to leave you behind for another group of friends? What if you never had to do anything to prove yourself because you had a friend who knew you inside and out and accepted you? What if you didn't have to be cool, or popular, or funny, or pretty, or smart because this friend loved you no matter what?

Jesus died for our sins and rose from the grave to make us his friends. If we've received his gift, then we already have a friend like no other. Having Jesus as our friend doesn't mean that human friendships aren't important—they are. But knowing he loves us changes everything. Our friends can be an extra blessing, not what our whole life depends on.

> **BOTH:** How do you know when friendships mean more to you than they should?

Understanding God's love for us helps us in many ways: When we want to talk about others, we can remember that God showed us mercy and we can show others mercy. When we want to keep people out, we can remember that Jesus died so that we could be pulled into his family. When we feel lazy, we can remember how much Jesus went through for us.

Instead of focusing on how we can get what we want from our friends, we can follow our Savior and look for ways to encourage, build up, include, bless, and love those around us. We can ask God to teach us how to be a friend like he is.

 THE FIELD

- **What are some characteristics of a wise friend? How can you be a wiser friend to those around you?**
- **What is something you are thankful for about mother-daughter friendships?**
- **Do you think of Jesus as a friend? What are some of the ways he has shown his friendship to you?**
- **Are there friends that pressure you to do bad things or look a certain way? How can you love people in your life who are acting like "fools" without being influenced by them?**

Walk 6
Our Appearance

Have you ever had a family photo taken and afterward everyone crams around, breathing down each other's necks, trying to get a glimpse of the picture? They all pretend they're examining the group, but who are they really checking out? Themselves! "Is my smile weird?" "Is my hair too frizzy?" "Am I happy with how I look?" That question is a common one for us, but can you imagine other parts of God's creation asking that: a group of prairie dogs comparing their height, the sun admiring its brilliance, a dandelion crying because she didn't have as many white fluffy things as her neighbor?

There is a public garden near my house that boasts a "flower walk." Every time I've been there, I've had to weave around photographers focusing their lenses and people crouched over velvety petals. In all their exclamations, I've never heard anyone comparing the flowers in a negative way: "Wow, look how dumpy that white daisy looks beside that yellow daffodil." "Check out that pathetic pink rose next to the dark red one." Never! What everyone loves is the variety. The differences only add to the beauty of the walk.

MOMS: What is the most beautiful place you have ever visited?

GIRLS: If you had to design a bouquet for a special occasion, what colors and flowers would you choose?

🌼 **THE GARDEN.** Like the gardeners who planted the flower walk, God is an artist who appreciates beauty. One look at the jeweled night sky or a towering oak proves that. And that same artist created you—with your red, black, blond, or brown waves, curls, or strands—and you are his idea of gorgeous.

Read Psalm 139:14–15.

We were made "fearfully and wonderfully." There is mystery in those words, almost as if something magical happened. Oh to watch, in fear and wonder, that Sculptor work, forming this face and those eyes and that body with precision. Each work is a masterpiece. I wonder if he walks down his own "Flower Walk" of people, noticing how the different shades of skin complement each other, smiling at the distinct eye shapes and colors, admiring the careful bone structure.

Did you notice the first three words in the passage? They were "I praise you." God made us amazingly, but that shouldn't make us focus only on the artwork; it should inspire praise for the Artist.

✳️ **THE WEEDS.** The world's perspective is different from God's. Beauty is for individual glory, and the weeds of pride and envy have grown up and hidden the loveliness of our differences. We too often compare ourselves with others and wish we could look a certain way. Almost everything on TV and movies and the Internet holds up a certain standard of beauty. There are even some women who have had surgery done to make them look like Barbie dolls!

GIRLS: If someone told you to close your eyes and picture a pretty girl, what would she look like?

MOMS: What did "pretty" hair and clothes look like when you were your daughter's age?

The pressure to look a certain way, be a certain size, and have the perfect skin produces serious problems. Girls think they're ugly: their shape is wrong; their hair, wrong; their skin, wrong. But they are wrong; God delights in each of his masterpieces and loves the way they look.

A different kind of weed that can pop up is the "I don't care" weed. If we can't look amazing, we'll just bag the whole thing. We'll stand out by not bothering. But this doesn't work. Greasy hair, a ripped shirt, and bad breath aren't going to attract anyone to us or to the God we serve. Taking care of ourselves by dressing neatly, exercising, and eating right is important. Finding the balance can be tricky, but we don't have to figure these things out by ourselves. Remember, God told moms to talk to their daughters when they rise, so early morning chats while you're brushing hair and getting dressed are all part of the plan. Get talking!

THE HILL. Remembering God's view of beauty can be difficult when the whole world is screaming that we have to look like the girl on the magazine cover. But Jesus died for you, and for the girl on that magazine, so that you could both be accepted by God. Because we belong to a loving Father, we don't have to sweat, strive, and strain to "belong" to the world. We don't need to look perfect. We can relax. We're his.

Sometimes, if we're honest with ourselves, that doesn't seem like enough and we still long to be accepted and admired. That's why we need to help each other believe the truth that God's view of us is the one that matters, and the only one that brings real peace and joy. We can also remind each other that there is another kind of prettiness that God values far more than the kind we see in the mirror, and it's available to everyone.

Read 1 Samuel 16:7b.

God is even more attracted to our inside beauty than our outside beauty.

First Peter 3:4 and Proverbs 31:30 describe the kind of "inside" God considers pretty.

Even better than movie star looks is having a gentle, quiet spirit that fears the Lord. Don't worry, "gentle and quiet" doesn't mean you need to turn into a mouse: it means that your heart quietly trusts the Lord and you respond gently to his leading. You can do all of those things with a fun, loud personality. Fearing him means that you have such respect for him that it changes the way you live. That is beauty to him.

MOMS: When have physical comparisons been difficult for you? How has God helped you focus on inward beauty?

GIRLS: Is it hard for you to think of yourself as a masterpiece? Do particular people make you feel more self-conscious about how you look?

Improving our outward appearance is fun. Doing hair, painting nails, and going shopping are all activities we can enjoy together.

Moms and daughters need each other to help them look their best. Let's always remember, though, that God has made us wonderfully, that lovely hearts are better than perfect faces, and that he loves us no matter what.

 THE FIELD

- **How do social media overemphasize appearance? Do you think people always look as good in real life as they make themselves look in their photos?**
- **Is completely forgetting about our appearance a good thing to do? Why or why not?**
- **Who can you encourage about their inner rather than outer beauty this week?**
- **Is there some aspect of your own appearance that you struggle with? Can anything you talked about today help with that struggle?**

"**D**id you have your quiet time today?"

"Well," you mumble, "I started to read my Bible, and then my eyelids somehow closed and that's all I remember. But I'm pretty sure it was quiet."

Spending daily time with Jesus can seem a little mysterious. If it's called a quiet time, why does it have to be so quiet? If it's called devotions, how do you "devote"? Are there rules? Are there prizes? Are there lightning strikes for forgetting? Do you get extra points if you pray on your knees on a hard floor? Do you lose points if you read your Bible snuggled in the nest of blankets in your bed?

> **MOMS:** What is the most unusual place you have ever had your quiet time?
>
> **GIRLS:** What do you think a "quiet time" or "devotional time" should look like?

🌼 **THE GARDEN.** Before we talk about "how to have a quiet time," let's consider how surprising it is that God actually wants to be in a relationship with us. This is the God who lit the stars, measures the oceans, and numbers the ants. The Bible says he turns the hearts of kings (Proverbs 21:1), and yet he loves to talk with us, even when we have bed head or a Fruity Pebble stuck to our chin.

He knows and loves his people and wants us to know and love him; but how? Is there a megaphone to the sky?

God has given us two main ways to know him and relate to him: the Bible (where God talks to us) and prayer (where we talk to God). Like any good conversation, it's great to experience them both together, but since they're both so important, we'll talk about the Bible in this walk and save the topic of prayer for the next one.

Let's start by looking at **Psalm 19:7–11**.

Did you think that frying bacon revives the soul? Nope, not like the Bible. Do you think textbooks make people wise? They're not even close to God's Word. Scripture brings wisdom, joy, light, and sweetness to our lives because it contains the very words of God.

Imagine God sitting at his heavenly desk, sipping whatever heavenly drink God sips, and writing you a letter. This letter would tell you how to know God and please him, what he thinks of you, and how to find true joy. After he signs his name, he hurls it down and it lands on the foot of your bed.

Read 2 Timothy 3:16.

God "breathed out" these words. They came directly from him. Now I'll admit that the words God gave us aren't in the form of a letter addressed specifically to you, and at first, they can seem difficult to figure out. But the Bible is actually a true story about God and how he has revealed himself over thousands of years. It's a story that tells us about ourselves as well, and how God rescued us from the mess we made. God has included us in the story because he loves us. In its pages, the Bible tells us of God's astonishing desire to be with his people even though they so often didn't want to be with him. His story includes songs, history, letters, promises, commands, and a victorious ending. The truths in this book will never pass away and are treasures worth digging for.

Your parents can help you read and understand the Bible, whether you're just starting out or have been at it for a while. Joshua 1:8 tells us to "meditate on it day and night" so that we can learn to obey it and receive blessings from God. So set aside a time each day to read a portion of God's Word, then ask yourself how you can apply what you read. Is there a command to obey? Is there a promise to remember? Is there a prayer to pray?

MOMS: What do you love about God's Word? Do you have a favorite Scripture?

✴ **THE WEEDS.** In any garden, weeds left to grow will strangle the life from plants trying to grow nearby. A weed that will suck the life out of your times with God is called legalism, and it means trying to earn God's love. When we're legalistic, we think that if we have our devotions, then God will love us more and make sure we have a good day. On the other hand, if we forget to read our Bibles for a while—uh-oh—we better lay low like the dog hiding behind the couch after he chewed the table leg. The master is not going to be happy. No treats tonight. It sounds sort of right, doesn't it, but it couldn't be more wrong. God loves us because of what Jesus did on the cross, not because of how well we obey.

Another weed whispers just the opposite: "God loves you no matter what, so you can stay snuggled in your bed and do what's easy. You don't need to seek him and worry too much about obeying; he will always be there for you." Oh, the blessings we lose by listening to that voice. We need God's help and grace and strength each day, and he delights to meet us in our times with him. Although our devotional times don't earn God's love, they do deepen our communion with him. God commands us to seek him, knowing that's where we will find true joy.

THE HILL. What Jesus did on the hill is humbling because it's free. There is nothing we can add to it. It shows us we're not good, but we're loved beyond our wildest imaginations. We're sinners who have been forgiven. The dirty rags of our sin and self-trust have been replaced with Jesus's clean white clothes. It shows us that whether we've read our Bibles for an hour and done one hundred good deeds, or gotten up late and had a terrible day, God loves us the same because of Christ. It's an amazing love that we can't earn. It shows us that God wants to be our Father, and we are always welcome to come to him. In light of that, we should be running to this wonderful Savior with thanksgiving, with questions, with sin struggles, or just for a moment together with him. And that's what quiet times are all about: coming to the one who made us and loves us.

Even though God loves to meet with us anywhere and anytime, it's wise to have a special time with God each day. It's like a little date. Girls, your mom and dad will guide you in this, but all you need is a time, a place, and a plan. Here is an example:

Time: 7:45 a.m.
Place: My purple beanbag chair
Plan: Read one section of Scripture in Mark and pray
    for five minutes.

Now it's your turn.

MOMS: What is your time, place, and plan?

GIRLS: What is yours? Write it out.

God wants to be with you. When it gets hard, tell him about it. Ask for his help. He loves to answer those prayers.

 THE FIELD

- Is it easier for you read God's Word or pray? Why do you think that is?
- Which of the following keeps you from devotional time: TV, sleeping in, phones or devices, homework, bad planning, lack of desire, or confusion about how to spend time with God?
- How can you help each other create and keep a daily quiet time?
- Are there are any "tools" that would help you (a devotional book, a prayer journal, a Bible)?
- What special reward can you share if you stick to your plans every day this week?

Walk 8
Our Prayers

Have you ever tried to talk to someone while you're in the shower? You're working shampoo through your hair and strike up a conversation with your sister who is brushing her teeth four feet away.

"Hey, I can't wait to go to the beach next week," you say. "Mom said it's going to be sunny."

No response.

"I want to make sure I remember that book I'm reading; and by the way, I can't find my beach towel," you continue. "Do you know where it is?"

No response.

"Hey, why aren't you answering?" you bellow, to which she snaps that she's been answering all the time, but all the running water and the soap in your ears prevented you from hearing.

One-sided conversations stink.

> **GIRLS:** Who, in your household, do you think could talk the longest without realizing no one was answering?

🍀 **THE GARDEN.** On our last walk we talked about reading the Bible. We learned that the Bible is breathed out by God, and that we should study and think about it regularly. Reading the Bible shows us God's will and God's ways. It's how he talks to us. But God doesn't like one-sided conversations either, which is pretty amazing because he has every right to speak and expect us to listen. He commands; we obey. He instructs; we follow. He teaches; we learn. Why would he want to listen to us too? Remarkably, God not only speaks, but also desires that we speak to him. Jesus himself gave us a lesson on how to talk to God.

Read Matthew 6:5–13.

Jesus tells us we shouldn't pray to sound spiritual or impress others, but we should remember that we are praying to our Father, who cares for us. We should do it simply and trustingly. He even gives us an example of a short prayer that praises God; submits to God's plan; and asks God for food, forgiveness, and protection from sin and evil. Those are great ideas of what to pray about in our own prayers. Our heavenly Father will not only listen to our prayers, but rewards us for praying them.

> **MOMS:** Describe a typical prayer of yours. Is it long or short? Does it follow a pattern? Have your prayers changed over the years?

Did you know that God filled one of the longest books of the Bible with prayers? Turn to the book of Psalms and flip the pages of all those chapters. Did you feel a breeze? Every single one of them is a prayer or song to God. Some were prayed through sobs in dark caves. Some were sung with bands and parades and dancing in the streets. Some were softly spoken on chilly nights as the psalmist admired the sparkling stars. God loves when we pour out our hearts to him, and he gave us the Psalms to teach us to pray. God wants to hear from us no matter where we are or what we're doing.

If you feel tongue-tied or uninspired, try praying through a psalm, adding your own words. Here is an example of how you might pray through Psalm 139:1–2:

> [The psalmist writes (verse 1):] *"O Lord, you have searched me and known me."*
>
> [You add:] Thanks that you know everything God. It's comforting, and a little scary too.
>
> [The psalmist writes (verse 2):] *"You know when I sit down and when I rise up; you discern my thoughts from afar."*
>
> [You add:] You know my thoughts of jealousy about that friend, Lord. Please help me to love her and to trust that what you've given me is enough.

BOTH: Do you see how it works? Turn to Psalm 139 and practice praying through verses 3–7 together. You'll be surprised how quickly you catch on.

THE WEEDS. Prayer is simple: Jesus showed us how. Prayer is a privilege: we get to talk to God himself. But praying is not always easy.

We battle distractions: There's a fly on the wall . . . God probably doesn't care about that argument with my friend anyway . . . Which cereal do I want for breakfast? . . . I can't think of anything to say . . . I feel sleepy . . .

We battle self-sufficiency: I'm doing a pretty good job managing my life. I don't really need God's help with anything today.

We battle laziness: Maybe I'll pray later. I don't know if I can concentrate now. I'll just read a chapter of my other book first.

We battle guilt: I've sinned so much lately. I've gotten in arguments and complained a ton and yelled at people. Why would God want to hear from me?

BOTH: What keeps you from prayer: distractions, self-sufficiency, laziness, guilt?

THE HILL. Something remarkable happened when Jesus breathed his last breath on the cross. "The curtain in the temple was torn in two, from top to bottom" (Matthew 27:51). The temple in Jerusalem was the center of worship for God's people. God's presence resided in an inner room known as the Most Holy Place, which was set apart from the Holy Place by a four-inch-thick curtain. For thousands of years, the message had been clear: God is holy and we are not; don't come near. Sinful people cannot come near to a holy God. In the temple, only the High Priest could enter God's presence, and then only once a year after much preparation.

When Jesus died, however, that thick curtain was miraculously ripped in two from top to bottom. Because Jesus had paid for their sins, God's people were welcome to enter into his very presence.

Read Hebrews 4:16.

Now, not only can we come before God's throne of grace, but we can come with confidence assured of receiving the mercy we seek. With such a sacrifice made for us, and such a God to come to, how can we stay away?

THE FIELD

- Do you feel like prayer is more of a privilege or a duty? Why?
- When you pray, do you feel invited in by God, or do you feel like you should stay far away? Did this study remind you of God's open arms?
- If you struggle to pray, consider doing it together occasionally. It can help to have a partner when you pray.
- If you didn't get a chance to make a devotional plan during the last walk, make one now, and ask each other every day how it's going.

Walk 9
Our Families

There is a special quality about family: no one bothers you more, and no one loves you more. Whether it's just one parent, or two parents and twenty siblings, these are people you can take for granted, depend on, run to, laugh with, wear your pajamas in front of, and absolutely belong to. Family is a priceless gift, created by someone very wise.

Now "priceless" might not be the first word that zings into your brain when you think of your family. Girls, you might think of your sister hogging all the covers at night or your brother making fun of your bed head. You might think of the chores your mom makes you do when you really don't want to and it wasn't even your turn. But make sure you also remember the cozy dinners, the encouragement, the warm hugs, and the love you receive from them.

MOMS: What is one family memory you have from when you were little?

GIRLS: What is your earliest memory of your family?

🌼 **THE GARDEN.** When God formed Adam from the dust of the earth, there was no companion for him. There were bears, skunks, eagles, and ladybugs, and God could have left it at that, but he gave Adam a wife, Eve. He gave them children and they shared life together. They ate, and slept, and hunted, and worked, and rested together. Family was God's idea, and just like everything else God made, it was good.

God told the waves how to crash, he told the sun how to shine, and he told family members how to relate to one another. (Notice how well the waves and the sun obey.)

Read Ephesians 6:1–3.

You've probably heard this passage before, and do I hear a sigh? Even though it can be hard to obey sometimes, the authority God has given parents is meant to be a blessing, and it honors the Lord.

Continue on to Ephesians 6:4.

There are instructions for parents too. God's desire is that we all walk humbly and kindly in the roles he has given us.

Our families, like everything God created, are meant to reflect him. That means they have the potential to be magnificent. Dads and moms have different qualities that show off different aspects of God's glory. Parents' warm love for their children mirrors God's love for us. Kids' happy responses to their parents bring joy to God, parents, and kids alike.

That all sounds great. So what's the trouble?

THE WEEDS. When the serpent tempted Adam and Eve in the garden, he basically said, "Hey, you don't need to listen to God's rules. He doesn't know what he's talking about. Nothing bad will happen if you disobey and do what you want." We know now that the serpent was lying. Lots of terrible things happened as a result of Adam and Eve's disobedience. Even today, disobedience to God's commands brings consequences.

GIRLS: How are you most tempted to disobey your mom and dad?

MOMS: What are some ways you exasperate your daughter?

BOTH: How do our wrong responses change the mood of our homes?

Because we're not perfect people, sometimes we have less than perfect thoughts about each other. We wish our family were as happy as our friend's family looks. We wish we got along better with our brother. We wish we had a sister closer to our age. We wish our parents were more fun and had more money. We wish everyone would be nicer to us. Notice how the weeds always point us back to what we want.

🔵 **THE HILL.** Even though Jesus had a family (and probably shared a room with snoring little brothers), he never gave in to the temptations that hounded him. He never sinned.

Read Matthew 20:28.

What was Jesus's purpose in coming to earth? What wasn't his purpose?

Jesus showed us a new way of living. He came to serve, not be served. He came to give, not to take. He came to sacrifice and love, and lay down his life for people like us. There is no way we could ever love our family members perfectly or erase our selfish thoughts and actions. So Jesus did. That verse we read a minute ago said that he became our ransom. That means he paid an immense price to free us from the prison of our sins, and that price was his life. It was agonizing and scary for Jesus to die for us, but he did it with joy because he loved us.

Because he threw those jail doors open for us, we're not prisoners of sin anymore. We can look at our families in a new way. They aren't just people we're stuck in the same house with; they are gifts from God whom we can serve and love, like Jesus did us.

It's easy to put on a good show with people outside our families. We smile politely and offer thoughtful comments. But the truth is that who we are at home with our families is who we really are. That's why it's so important to start there, and look for ways to honor God in our own homes. God loves to help us when we're weak, and he loves to give us grace when we feel like we can't obey. Just ask him.

Each member of your family has been handpicked by God for you—yes, even that one. Each is God's perfect choice. As you choose to love them, you'll realize it brings joy. Selfishness is a gray jail cell. Love is a wide-open field under a blue sky.

> **GIRLS:** What is one suggestion you have for how your mom could serve your family this week in a creative way?
>
> **MOMS:** What is one suggestion you have for how your daughter could love the family this week?

God loves family because he has his own. He is our loving heavenly Father, and if we receive his gift of salvation, we are his cherished daughters whom he promises to keep, love, protect, provide for, and cherish forever.

THE FIELD

- List ten things you're thankful for about your family.
- Can you think of a TV show or movie that shows kids and parents interacting? Does it show kids obeying or disobeying their parents? Does it make the parents look wise or foolish?
- Why do you think that family is important to God?
- When does your family get along best together? When do they get along worst? Is there a way you could act in that situation that would help rather than hinder family interactions?

Walk 10
Our Weaknesses

The females in my family line have an odd disorder. I can't seem to find it in the medical books, and I don't think it has an official name, but here it is: We can't do cartwheels. It's shocking, I know. I was surprised by it when I was little and every neighborhood girl I knew would cartwheel across the lawn like a runaway wagon wheel. My sister and I were in good shape, but our attempts at cartwheels ended in heaps.

Our cartwheel disorder sounds like a small thing, and it was, but when everyone is taking turns doing them in gym class, it feels like a pretty big deal. We don't usually like our weaknesses. They are things to be hidden. "Oh no," we assure, as we wander coolly away, "I just don't feel like doing a cartwheel right now."

BOTH: What are two things you are really bad at?

THE GARDEN. We all have weaknesses. Some of us struggle in school, some of us get lost when we leave our driveway, and some of us are shy and awkward when we talk to people. We hate these weaknesses, but would it surprise you to learn that God likes them? The apostle Paul tells us about a personal struggle he had with weakness. He called it a "thorn" in the flesh (2 Corinthians 12:7). It might have been a sickness or a vision problem, but nobody knows for sure. It could have been anything. He pleaded with the Lord three times to take this weakness away.

Read 2 Corinthians 12:9–10.

God said to Paul, "Nope, I'm going to let this weakness remain so you can see my power at work, and so that others will know it's not *your* strength at work, but mine." It's almost as if God is setting Paul up to see God's strength and power and show it to others. Do you know what Paul does? Instead of whining, he joyfully boasts in his weaknesses. "Hey everybody, I really am weak. I can't hide it. But look at all God's done. His strength is working through me." Paul didn't need to pretend he had it all together. He found contentment in his weaknesses because they were spotlights on God's power in his life.

> **GIRLS:** How do you think God could show his power through one of the weaknesses you mentioned above?

✳ **THE WEEDS.** Do you, like Paul, boast about your weaknesses? It's harder than it sounds. A big thistle called pride is not going to stand for it. Let's take a closer look at pride and humility.

Read Philippians 2:3–4.

Whew, that's tough. Our pride wants to look only to our own interests. It wants us to be known for our strengths, not our weaknesses. That thistle comes in lots of varieties. Sometimes pride is easy to spot, like when we brag or bring up conversations about things we're good at, or when we smile smugly when we get a right answer. Other times it's hidden, like when we quietly think how much better we are than others or when we're upset because we aren't receiving the attention we want. When we're proud, we resent our weaknesses because they prove we don't have it all together.

> **MOMS:** As you remember your youth, what areas of foolish pride stand out? The more embarrassing the better.

Humility, according to those same verses, is counting "others more significant than yourselves." It's getting ourselves out of the center and loving others. It's celebrating someone else's accomplishments, not minding too much if we're overlooked, and laughing at our own mistakes. When we're humble, our weaknesses don't surprise us because we're not that impressed with ourselves anyway.

Humble people not only admit they're weak, but they confess their sins. Weaknesses aren't necessarily our fault, but sins are choices we make to disobey God. It's hard to say, "Please forgive me; I was wrong," but it's how we follow Jesus. You'll be surprised how good it feels afterward, and how attractive humility is to others.

> **GIRLS:** Describe a time when you noticed someone being humble.

THE HILL. The Philippians 2 passage we're reading continues by giving us an incredible example—a pinch-yourself-to-see-if-you're-dreaming kind of example.

Read Philippians 2:5–11.

Did you fall off your chair in shock? You read it right: Jesus, the prince of heaven with all the universe at his disposal, threw it all in. He emptied himself. He laid down his scepter and his dazzling robes and became an ordinary human being. He left behind strength and picked up weakness. The angels must have covered their eyes in horror.

As if that wasn't dreadful enough, the prince humbled himself further, even to the point of death. He hung in disgrace and shame on a cross with bystanders gawking and taunting. The prince was weak and frail. Do you know why? It was because he was looking to our interests, not his own. He knew we needed a perfect Savior, so he ignored his own reputation, and did the unthinkable for us. He gave us his life. His "weakness" showed us God's strength, love, and beauty.

What happened then? God exalted Jesus, honoring him above all. And here's one more crazy truth. Find out what it is in Matthew 23:12.

If we humble ourselves, God promises to exalt us too. We don't have to pretend we're strong and hide our weaknesses. The only way we can come to Jesus is to admit we're sinners, so our sins and weaknesses shouldn't surprise us. We can rejoice that although we will never be powerful and perfect, he is. And that's all we need to know.

 THE FIELD

- **What weakness do you find yourself being defensive or self-conscious about? How could our conversation today change that?**
- **Where do you find your identity? ("I'm important because I'm a good swimmer," or "I'm smart," or "I have a lot of friends," etc.)**

- What are some of the strengths of the people close to you? How could you forget about yourself and make a big deal about those strengths this week?
- Are there ways that pride has used its thorns to damage your mom-daughter relationship? Do you speak more humbly or more proudly with each other?

In the original Disney version of *Cinderella*, some mice befriend poor, overworked Cinderella and try to help her bear her heavy load. Perched on her broom handle, they sing in squeaky little voices of the jobs their gentle friend must do: making the fire, fixing breakfast, washing dishes, mopping and sweeping and dusting . . . the list seems endless!

Oh, those nasty stepsisters who lay around batting their eyelashes and barking orders at Cinderella. It must be nice to never have to work.

MOMS: Describe the worst work you ever had to do.

GIRLS: What is your favorite, and least favorite, household chore?

When you think of work, girls, you might think of offices or laptops or worst of all, your tornado of a room that needs be cleaned. Why talk about that? Isn't it more fun to talk about what we do *after* our work is done?

The real question is this: Is work, whatever it is, just something we're stuck with, like a runny nose, or does it have meaning?

🧩 **THE GARDEN.** Let's head into the garden and see if we can dig up an answer.

Read Genesis 2:2–3.

If you read the first chapter of Genesis, you will see that God did some important work. If God had reclined in his hammock a day early (the day before he made us), we wouldn't be having this conversation; in fact, we wouldn't be here. But really, who would mind working if it meant creating the Amazon River and bringing kangaroos to life? God's work sounds fun, but what about us? Does our work count?

Genesis 2 goes on to show us God instructing Adam to work and keep the garden, and creating Eve to be his helper. To God, work wasn't a punishment; it was a gift, and something that belonged in a perfect place. God knew the value and satisfaction of working and tending—whether gardens, babies, money, schoolwork, businesses, or homes. There is no work too menial or boring to reflect God and bring glory to him.

MOMS: Can you think of a time when you felt great satisfaction for a job well done?

GIRLS: What would your dream job be?

Read Colossians 3:23–24 to find out *how* we should work, whether we're doing our dream job or not.

"Whatever" is a wide word. Is it wide enough to include cleaning the toilet? Writing a science paper? Picking up, yet again, a giant pile of toys? Yes to all three—and everything else. You are doing it "for the Lord Christ." It's all noticed by God, who gives our work eternal value.

✳ **THE WEEDS.** When Adam and Eve sinned, one of the consequences was that their work became hard; weeds grew and plants got diseases. Work is still hard. On top of that, we have an enemy who wants to turn any joy in our work into complaining; eagerness to laziness; and helpfulness to selfishness. Our sinful nature (the part of us that always thinks of ourselves first) says, "Hey, I don't want to work. I want someone to work for me." Laziness yips at our heels. It doesn't just mean you're lying around playing video games; it can mean you're doing something good—but not the good thing you're supposed to be doing.

BOTH: When do you find yourself most tempted to do something other than what you should be doing?

Lazy people are great at making excuses. Do any of these sound familiar?
- **"I'm coming!" (accompanied by no movement)**
- **"I just need a few more minutes. I'm in the middle of something."**
- **"I'm really tired."**
- **"It's not my turn. I did it last time."**
- **"I don't know how."**

Excuses are easy to give when we don't want to work, but they do have consequences.

Read Proverbs 20:4.

Why are we reading about the sluggard? This is a practical verse about farming, but it can be applied to any area of life. If we don't finish our homework, we'll want good grades but won't have them. If we don't feed our animals, we'll want happy pets but won't have them. If we don't empty the dishwasher, we'll want clean spoons but won't have them. There is a logic here that we can't escape: hard workers receive reward and lazy ones don't.

 THE HILL. We've heard the story of the cross and the grave so often, we can go into a mindless "Uh-huh" mode and miss the hugeness of it all. What Jesus did that day absolutely flooded our lives with meaning. Light and hope and purpose poured down from heaven, filling every dark, dreary crack and crevice of our lives. You might say that Jesus reversed the curse that sin brought. Now we can do our work for the Lord, knowing that it honors him and has meaning. He notices it all and will even reward us for working hard. Every task has immeasurable, eternal value. That puts science papers, jobs, and tedious chores in a whole new light.

THE FIELD

- When you do chores, are you more likely to be singing, complaining, looking like a zombie, or chatting? Ask each other.
- What work do you have coming up this week that you're not looking forward to? What truth from our walk today could change your attitude about it?
- Surprise each other this week with a reminder note that God is glorified in our work. It could be hidden in the laptop, folded in the dishrag, or taped to a rake. Use your imaginations.
- Name a job that you could do for a family member or friend this week to surprise them, knowing that your work is done for God as well as for that person.

Walk 12
Our Church

As we're limbering up for our hike today, let's play a word game. I'll say a word, and you describe the scene that pops into your head as quickly as you can.

> **GIRLS:** You go first. Your word is *airplane*. Close your eyes and picture a scene, then describe it.

Did you say something about a jumbo jet roaring into the air, taking you to Disney World?

> **MOMS:** Your turn. Your word is *camping*. Describe your scene.

Chances are, your scene had something to do with swarms of mosquitoes and a soggy sleeping bag, but I could be wrong.

Now what if I said the word *church*? What scene immediately comes to mind? A group of kids talking in the lobby? A pastor delivering a sermon? A Sunday school classroom? An uncomfortable pew? Lunch afterward?

All those pictures are great. Friends, pastors, and even lunch come from God's generous hand, but did you ever wonder how Jesus views the church?

THE GARDEN. When Jesus plays this game and gets the word *church*, he doesn't think of a steeple, he thinks of a stunning bride—his bride—dressed in white and smiling down the aisle toward him. Have you ever been to a wedding and watched the groom as the bride comes down the aisle? His expression is usually one of wonder and delight. Does it surprise you to learn that the church is the bride of Christ? The expression on the groom's face is a picture of how Christ sees his church. That's how much he loves her.

Let's look for some other scenes that come to Jesus's mind.

Read 1 Peter 2:9.

This verse gives us some important-sounding titles that show just how special the church is to God. It also reveals the church's purpose to "proclaim the excellencies of him who called you out of darkness into his marvelous light." Our job as members of Christ's church is to tell how amazing Jesus is and all that he's done for us.

Another picture that would come to Jesus's mind is a tall, white pillar. **Read 1 Timothy 3:15** to find out what this pillar is holding up.

It's the truth. The church holds up the precious, priceless truth of God. We can often think of church as just a thing we do or a place we go. But everything that goes on there—the singing, preaching, caring, encouraging, praying, helping, and teaching—helps hold up the weighty truth we talked about. The Bible tells us that the church is a very big deal to God, and a great honor to be part of. He cherishes her, and she glorifies him. Your own church is a part of that, whether it's tiny or huge, loud or quiet, rural or urban, ancient or modern. Your very own church is the bride of Christ.

✳ **THE WEEDS.** Maybe the scene you pictured wasn't full of pillars and brides and "marvelous light." Maybe it was full of boredom, feeling out of place, confusing Bible verses, or long sermons. Weeds even grow up through the church floor sometimes. Instead of reminding each other of God's kindness, we begin to speak unkindly about each other. Instead of considering the words of the songs we're singing, we think about how terrible the person behind us sings. Instead of asking, "Do I help the church?" we ask, "Do I like the church? Does it entertain me?"

MOMS: Are you ever tempted to forget how much God adores the church and, instead, reflect more on its weaknesses?

GIRLS: What are you most grateful for about your church? What are you most distracted by in church?

🔵 **THE HILL.** You might be wondering why we're spending a whole walk discussing the church. Isn't that something other people should be thinking about? Aren't there pastors and deacons and other dignified people who can do all that stuff in an elders' meeting? The answer to that question is yes and no. Yes, God has called certain people to lead the church, but no, it's not just for them. Jesus died and rose again not just to save us from death, but to make us a family who can show the world what his love looks like.

We're all part of it. You're part of it. The old woman with the shrill voice behind you is part of it. Your older brother or husband in his basketball shoes is a part of it. Your pastor, your parents, your children, your friends are a part of it. Throw yourself in because you have a part to play. All you need is a heart that loves Jesus and wants to help. You can play with a toddler while his mom is in a conversation. You can sit beside the newcomer who doesn't know anybody. You can pick up items people have left behind after the service. You can thank your teachers and pastors. You can smile at a guest. You can sing during worship. You can listen closely to the message. All of these acts of love bring a smile to our Savior's face as he cherishes his bride.

GIRLS: What are some ways you have served your church, and what are some new ways you could try?

MOMS: What is one way that you need the church and the church needs you?

Sometimes going to church is like biting into a steaming slice of pizza, and sometimes it's more like eating a bowl of oatmeal. Both fill you up, but one is a little more enjoyable. That's OK. God can still nourish you even when church doesn't seem that exciting.

Read Hebrews 10:24–25.

Stir one another up. Encourage one another. Keep reminding each other that Jesus is real, that he loves his bride, and that he will come back for her. When you open the church door, you might not hear angels singing or see a ray of light shining down from heaven onto your pastor. You might just smell pine cleaner and hear the clatter of chairs being set up. The people you meet might seem pretty ordinary. But remember, this unimpressive group—meeting in this unimpressive building—are, in God's eyes, "a chosen race, a royal priesthood, a holy nation, a people for his own possession." Now that's special.

THE FIELD

- It's easy to take our churches for granted. What are some specific ways your church is like a pillar, holding up the truth?
- Try praying for your church together each night this week, and see how that affects your hearts on Sunday.
- This Sunday, look for someone new or lonely to reach out to. You can start a conversation with them, sit with them, or invite them to an upcoming event.
- Name someone who helps hold up the truth and keep your church going. Text or e-mail them right now to thank them for all they do.

I've always had a thing for Volkswagen Beetles. Maybe you call them VWs or Punch Buggies. They're little cars shaped like gumdrops, usually painted bright colors, and they (at one time anyway) made a puttering sound when they went by. When I was a child, my family had a blue one, then a red one, and my first car was a bright yellow one with a racing steering wheel. I thought it was pretty cool.

When I met the man who would be my husband, he drove a monster of a car called an Impala. I think its hood was longer than my entire little yellow Bug. A grown man could probably stretch out comfortably in the backseat. I could barely get in my backseat. The first time he drove my Bug, he ripped the handle right off the door.

Our cars got us where we wanted to go. They each ran well, had unique benefits, and not a little peeling paint; but they were designed very differently. That's what made them fun.

> **GIRLS:** If you could design your own car, what would it look like?

🌻 **THE GARDEN.** Males and females are designed differently. Have you noticed? They have tons in common, but there are some significant differences.

> **BOTH:** List five differences that come to mind.

Some differences you might have mentioned are always true, like body structure; and some are often true, like boys wrestling or girls playing with dolls. Although there is a lot of variation, there are some obvious differences between groups of little boys and girls, and the same goes for grown-ups. So which one is better?

Well, which was better, my husband's Impala or my Bug? It's an impossible question. They were both designed purposefully to be what they were. The Impala was smooth, but the Bug could zip around. Ranking them would be silly.

Read Genesis 1:27.

God created male and female in his own image. That means they are equally valuable but reflect God's character in different ways. A dad protecting his family from danger is a picture of God's protection of us. A mom comforting her child shows how God comforts us. Of course, sometimes moms protect and dads comfort, but they do these things according to their design.

The Bible says that a husband's humble leadership of his family shows God's leadership of the church and a wife responding to that leadership shows how the church responds to Christ. Our lives paint pictures.

The Bible doesn't tell us exactly how every woman's life should look, or every man's either. But it does tell us a lot. Proverbs 31 alone gives us a description of a godly woman as being worth more than a treasure chest of diamonds. Take turns reading verses 10–31.

This woman cares for the needs of her husband, her family, those outside her family, and herself as well. She is capable and trustworthy, making business decisions and working hard. She is wise, strong, and admirable, but she fears the Lord and trusts him enough to laugh at the future instead of worrying about it. It's an impressive picture of dedication and love.

THE WEEDS. I'm glad nobody took the Bug and the Impala, melted them down, and gave us two identical, medium-sized gray cars. What a bore. Sometimes it seems like that's what's happening with men and women in our world, and boys and girls too. People are afraid that differences mean that one is more important than the other, so they pretend we are all exactly the same, and that is one of the biggest weeds we encounter on this walk.

> **MOMS:** What are some ways you've seen this change happening?

Proverbs shows us godly women can do all kinds of things like running businesses and buying land, but the Bible gives wives special responsibility to care for their families and homes, and husbands special responsibility to lead (Titus 2:3–5). These roles are a privilege. Raising a family or creating a welcoming home is incredibly important but may make us nervous because we often picture life like a ladder. On the top rung are leaders who have lots of people to boss around, and on the muddy bottom rung are people who serve others and are unnoticed. We work hard to make sure we are near the top and wrinkle our noses at those low rungs. But here is something that might surprise you. Our ladder is upside-down.

Read Matthew 23:11–12.

Are you feeling dizzy? Is your ladder flipping? This verse says that on God's ladder, the highest rung is reserved for those who serve, no matter who they are. This means we don't need to worry about who is more important, or who makes the most money, or who can read faster, or who can jump higher. We don't need to be nervous about the differences. We are called to love and serve one another in all we do; that's the top rung of God's ladder.

Girls, your mom might care for your family excellently while working outside your home, or she might feel that staying home is the way she can do that best. Your dad might work at an office, or work from home, or be unable to work at all for some reason. God doesn't give us an exact description of what husbands and wives should do, but he does give us the pattern, and when we value what he values, we can trust him every step of the way.

GIRLS: What do you love most about being a girl? Is there anything you find difficult about it?

MOMS: What do you love most about being a woman? How would you encourage your daughter to grow in godly girlhood?

THE HILL. God made you a girl and your brother a boy for his own reasons, and who you are is a gift. God doesn't make mistakes. Your differences delight him, and it's comforting to know our wise God made that choice. God made us male and female, and gave his very life for us both. His costly sacrifice erases any question of who is more valuable and replaces it with a desire to be a person whose life honors him in every way.

Creation shows us that God made men and women differently with great purpose and design. The gospel shows that we each have dignity and worth. May our lives show that we trust his wisdom and delight in who he has made us.

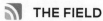 THE FIELD

This is a broad topic to cover in one walk. Some of you may be out of breath. If you'd like to spend more time on the topic, consider taking next week to discuss the "Field" questions below. They will guide you on a hike that will be worth the effort.

- **How do you see God's good design in creating male and female?**
- **Titus 2:3–5 lists six qualities that older women are to teach younger women. We're touching on many of them during our walks together. Moms, which of these six qualities would you like to grow in? Girls, which one do you most need your mom's help in?**
- **Do you think guys or girls have it better? How would Matthew 23:11–12 influence your feelings?**
- **Read through Ephesians 5:22–33, which describes one of the ways husbands and wives should interact. How could obedience to this command be beautiful and display God's glory? How could it be used wrongly, not reflecting God at all?**
- **In what ways can you encourage your brothers and male friends in godly manhood?**

Walk 14
Our Role Models

Abag of hand-me-downs is a treasure chest waiting to be opened. Oh, the potential, the hopes, the opportunities, the perfect outfits that might be hidden in there! Maybe they came from expensive stores; maybe the tags are still on them; maybe they're all the perfect size!

> **GIRLS:** Did you ever strike gold in a bag of hand-me-downs? What was the piece of clothing you loved the most?

Just like clothes are handed down, values are handed down. We watch the way others act, and dress, and speak, and we often want to be like them. Sometimes our role models are TV or movie stars, or singers, or girls in magazines. They have the hair we love or they seem to have fun wherever they go. Maybe they're skilled at the sport or musical instrument we play. There are all kinds of reasons we look up to others; and whether we are aware of it or not, there are others who look up to us.

THE GARDEN. God designed it that way. He wants children to look up to their parents and learn from them (Proverbs 1:8). He wants younger women to be taught godliness by older women

(Titus 2). He wants young Christians to study the lives of mature ones.

> **MOMS:** Who have you learned the most from?

Read 1 Corinthians 11:1 and 3 John 11.

What word do these verses have in common?

Did you find the word *imitate*? It might surprise you to know that we are supposed to imitate people, but not just anybody. We should only imitate others as they follow Christ. Like pawing through a rumpled bag of hand-me-downs, we are to keep the good stuff and pitch the bad. By watching for grace in others, we can discover role models all around us. In fact, let's spend some time figuring out whom we can be learning from.

> **BOTH:** As you read the following categories, each of you name the person who comes to mind. Include people from church, the neighborhood, school, your family—you get the idea.

- **Someone who always speaks kindly about others**
- **Someone who reaches out to younger kids**
- **Someone who works or studies hard and gets a lot done**
- **Someone who serves behind the scenes**
- **Someone who is friendly**
- **Someone who creates a cozy, inviting home or room**
- **Someone who can keep a secret**

- **Someone who always has yummy food to share**
- **Someone who can laugh at herself**
- **Someone who knows the Bible well**

Look at all the great examples you have in your life. And you may not even have known they were there. But girls, don't forget that the primary role model God has given you is your mom. I bet you could have put her name under lots of the categories above, and she is available to you all the time—no appointment necessary.

☀ **THE WEEDS.** God has planted fragrant examples all around us, but sometimes we walk right by instead of stopping to examine them. We don't always want to learn to speak gently or reach out to others. How about being popular? How about being pretty? How about being involved in fun activities, or shopping at the nice stores, or being funny? At least that's what our hearts can tell us— and that goes for both daughters and moms. Growing older doesn't mean we are done with these weeds. We still have to fight them off.

Read 1 John 2:15–17.

The things the world values will pass away: money, looks, charm, popularity, talent. It's hard to believe, but ask your mom. Looks fade, fashions change, popularity dwindles, wealth disappoints. They just can't bring lasting joy, but following Jesus can. Don't be fooled by the role models the world offers you. Search for the ones who imitate Christ, then imitate them. That's called wisdom.

> **GIRLS:** In what area have you been tempted to follow the world instead of Christ? Who is someone you could learn from in that area?

THE HILL. Jesus is the greatest role model of all, and throughout the Bible, he tells us to follow him. But he's much more than an example: He's the Savior. Jesus knew we wouldn't follow him perfectly, or even close to perfectly. None of the wonderful people you listed above follow him perfectly. The person you admire most in the world doesn't follow him perfectly. We all get tangled up in the weeds. Jesus knew that, so he gave his spotless life for us and snapped off those thorny tendrils that tie us to the world. In Galatians 2:20, Paul says: "I have been crucified with Christ. It is no longer I who live but Christ who lives in me." That means that our old self has died, and now Christ lives in us, calling us to follow him.

We couldn't ask for a better guide. He never asks us to do something he hasn't done. He's shown us how to love the unlovely, how to care for the sick, how to hate sin and love righteousness, how to suffer well, how to put others before ourselves, and how to obey our Father in everything. I'm so grateful we aren't alone. Jesus is our example, and he's given us our parents, the church, and godly friends to learn from. What a joy to follow God together.

THE FIELD

- Is there someone in the above list that you would like to learn from more purposefully? How could you do that?
- Do you have any role models or "heroes" who aren't helping you follow Christ?
- Each of you choose one person in the above list and jot them a quick note. Yes, right now. Use a napkin if that's all you have. They will be so encouraged.
- Who learns from you or looks up to you? How can you be a godly example to that person this week or reach out to them in some way?

Walk 15
Our World

I thought we'd begin our walk today at Niagara Falls. There's a 165-foot drop over the edge, so we'll have to be careful, and you might want to grab a raincoat because the spray will be pretty intense. If you're daring enough, we could try to walk across the falls on a tightrope. It's only a 1,800-foot, windy walk over tons of crashing, swirling water. Would you do it? A few years ago a man named Nik Wallenda completed this feat with the help of a 30-foot-long balancing pole. When he leaned too far one way, he'd lean the balancing pole the other way to steady himself. It was crazy, and the tightrope was swinging in the wind, but he made it, kissing the ground on the other side when he reached it.

GIRLS: How do you think you would do walking a tightrope way up high? What's the highest you've been? Did you get a weird feeling in your stomach when you looked down?

The walk we're taking today won't be on a tightrope, but it will be on a very narrow path. We could easily slip and tumble off into the weeds on either side, so don't forget your balancing pole, the Bible.

THE GARDEN. The question we'll be tossing around as we hike is, "How should Christians interact with the world around them?" Do we take our Bible and a few sandwiches into a cave and peek out with a suspicious eye every few hours? Do we run headlong into the crowd and dive into whatever activity is going on? Let's hear God's instructions on the topic.

Read Romans 12:1–2, paying particular attention to the beginning of verse 2.

God commands us, "Do not be conformed to this world." Those words aren't forbidding us to turn into a planet and grow grass and sprout trees; they're warning us to resist getting sucked into the sinful values around us. If a clique at school is insulting someone, don't become like them. If a TV show is making sin look fun, turn it off. If an ad tells you it's *impossible* to be happy without that new look, don't believe it. God is saying, "Be careful to follow Jesus, not the world around you."

MOMS: What part of the world can suck you in if you're not careful? What sucked you in when you were younger?

God doesn't want us to blindly jump into everything our world offers, but he doesn't want us to hide from it either. The Bible instructs us several times to love others as we love ourselves. Now, you might not think you love yourself all that much, but do you fix yourself a snack when you're hungry? Do you like compliments? Do you spread nasty rumors about yourself? Most of us love and serve ourselves very faithfully, and that's exactly how much we're to love people around us.

First Corinthians 13:4–7 offers us a deeper look at what love looks like. Check it out.

What a list! Read it again, replacing the word *love* with your own name. Is that a good description of you? Are you patient and kind, not envying or boasting, not arrogant or rude, not insisting on your own way, not irritable or resentful, not rejoicing in wrongdoing, but rejoicing in the truth? Do you bear, believe, hope, and endure all things? I know it doesn't sound enough like me, but it's a beautiful picture of how we should treat people.

BOTH: Which one of these phrases is the most difficult for you?

THE WEEDS. Remember that narrow path we said we'd be navigating? When we're figuring out how to deal with situations in the world around us, it's easy to fall into the thorns of self-righteousness on one side and the thistles of worldliness on the other.

Self-righteousness tells us that we're better than others, and we would never do something bad like they did. It makes us forget that we're all sinners. Christians aren't naturally good people: just the opposite. Christians realize they were lost in their sin and Jesus graciously forgave them. But self-righteousness makes it about "us" and "them."

On the other side of the path, worldliness tells us to forget God's commands and do as the world does. If the world mocks, join in the mockery. If the world wastes time, do what they do. It tells us to blend in and do what works; after all, God is a forgiving God, isn't he?

Let's say there is a squabble in the neighborhood. One girl says she doesn't like you because you're annoying and your parents have dumb rules, and she gossips about you to some of the other kids. Situations like that hurt terribly, and we can find ourselves stuck in self-righteousness, thinking, *How can she act like this? I would never stoop so low. She's mean and I don't even want to be friends.* Or, we jump to the other side and spread gossip about her to get revenge. Staying on the path of love—being patient, enduring, and hoping for the best—requires lots of grace. Fortunately, God loves to give it.

GIRLS: Now you try it. Let's say all your friends are talking about a movie that has all kinds of things in it that dishonor God. What does staying on the path of love look like? How could we fall off either side?

MOMS: Your turn. Imagine that a neighbor finds out you follow the Bible on a particular issue, but she strongly disagrees and calls you narrow-minded and judgmental. How could you respond well, and what would falling off the two sides look like for you?

THE HILL. It takes courage to stand up for righteousness. Our world doesn't always like the idea that certain things are right or wrong; it wants to do as it pleases. It won't usually congratulate us on our attempts to follow God. It won't say, "Good job not conforming to us," and it may even dislike us. Jesus's world certainly didn't love him, but he loved anyway. Jesus was always patient and kind. He never envied or boasted. He wasn't arrogant or rude, didn't insist on his own way, and wasn't irritable or resentful. He didn't rejoice in wrongdoing, but rejoiced in the truth. Jesus bore all things, believed all things, hoped all things, and endured all things. He loved the sinner and reached out to the unlovely. He embraced dirty people and healed the diseased. But he never adopted their ways. He led them to a much better way.

Jesus can help us do the same. We all naturally put ourselves first, but Jesus not only conquered our selfishness on the cross, he also gave us the Holy Spirit to help us love. In fact, Romans 5:5 tells us, "God's love has been poured into our hearts through the Holy Spirit who has been given to us." So we aren't stuck with our own meager amount of love. God shares his love with us, so we can do what we couldn't do in our own strength. We can love when we feel angry. We can lead others in what's right when we feel weak. We can follow God when it would be a whole lot easier to follow the world.

Even when it gets hard and we feel alone, we can rejoice. Do you know why? **Read Matthew 5:11–12** to find out.

Jesus has you, and he will never forsake you. If you stand for him, your reward will be great. You can count on it.

 THE FIELD

- Are there situations where you are sliding into the self-righteous side of the path? What changes need to be made?
- Are there any situations where you are sliding into the worldly side of the path? What changes need to be made?
- Are there media that pull you into the world too much? (TV, social media, Internet shopping, music, movies, etc.)
- Remember the characteristic of 1 Corinthians 13 you said was hard for you? What are three specific ways you could grow in that this week? Check in with each other in a few days to see how it's going.

Walk 16
Our Changes

Some of us like change, and some of us don't.
If you rearrange your bedroom every other week, beg for permission to paint the walls for the tenth time, and doze off in wildly different positions each night, you might like change. But . . . if you can't sleep without your piggy Pillow Pet tucked behind your left shoulder, your crocheted blanket folded carefully over your stomach, and your mom's ten-minute singing-praying-hugging-kissing ritual, you might not like change too much. It's just a guess.

Like it or not, we do change. Our minds change, our bodies change, our feelings change, our relationships change, and our tastes change. For those of you in a nervous sweat, I can assure you that eye color usually doesn't change, but that's about it. It's a good thing too because growing up is one of the most exciting things you will ever get to do.

GIRLS: From the description above, do you think you like change or not? Why?

MOMS: What was the biggest change in your life? How did you handle it?

❀ THE GARDEN. Growing up can feel complicated, but God provides us simple wisdom that will keep us grounded. **Read 2 Timothy 3:14–15** to find out what it is.

No matter how many emotions, friends, sets of braces, and shoe sizes you move through, hang onto the truth you've been taught and keep studying and applying God's Word to your life. It will anchor you in the midst of the waves. But even with a firm anchor, you'll still have all kinds of questions arise. That's why God has given you parents to help you figure it all out. Talking isn't always easy though. When moms initiate a conversation, they may receive the dreaded eye roll or their daughter jamming a pillow over her head. When girls hint that they have a question, moms might miss it and say, "Sure honey, let's talk later," and later never happens. So let's jump right in, shall we?

Your body will change over the next few years, or maybe it has already. Suddenly your favorite shorts are too short, and your T-shirts don't hang the same way. You need to wash your hair more often, and your skin isn't quite as smooth as it used to be. You notice that some of your friends look like women and some still look like young girls, and you're not sure which camp you want to be in. Part of you finds it exciting and is drawn to grown-up styles, and part of you wants to hold onto your teddy bear for dear life. Sometimes girls' feelings are so bottled-up that they can't sleep. No matter how wild and crazy your feelings are, it's important to share them with your mom. She has been there.

Read Psalm 18:30, paying particular attention to the first sentence.

Whether growing up is happening too quickly or too slowly for you, God's way—in the huge things and the small—is perfect. He knows exactly what you need.

> **GIRLS:** Is the idea of growing up more exciting or scary? Is there anything your mom could do to make talking about it easier?

How you feel about boys often changes during these years as well. Some of your friends are starting to talk about them differently, and maybe you are too. Maybe one of your friends likes a guy, or she's trying to match you up with someone. All these changes are signs that your mind and body are growing in healthy ways, but you need to be careful that you don't run too far too fast.

Read Paul's advice to his young friend Timothy in **1 Timothy 4:12**.

Even as young people, we're to set an example in all these areas, including purity. Being pure means keeping our hearts clean from the stains of the world by obeying God's commands. We stay pure by guarding our minds from sinful images, our ears from crude talk, our minds from unclean thoughts, our bodies from inappropriate action.

God's gift of marriage and romance is a thrilling one. Imagining your wedding day and wondering who you'll marry are happy daydreams. You can even start to pray now for your future husband. Look forward to enjoying the gift of marriage and romance when the time is right, but be sure not to rush it by jumping into romantic relationships too early. God's Word tells us that certain aspects of romance are reserved for marriage, so we need to walk wisely in this area, remembering that sometimes the best things in life are the things we wait for. Enjoy your changing feelings for boys in purity by treating them with kindness. Pursue friendship rather than flirtation. How wonderful if they do the same for us.

MOMS: Describe the moment you knew that you were going to marry your husband.

GIRLS: Is there anything or anyone in your life that is tempting you toward impurity or unwrapping the gift of romance too early? It could be a conversation with a friend, something you saw on the Internet, or a friendship with a particular boy. Is there anything your mom can help you with? Don't hide.

※ **THE WEEDS.** Weeds spread quickly. They crowd around a new bean sprout until you have to look hard to differentiate the plant from the weeds. It's hard to stay pure in the world we live in. When our bodies begin changing, fear reaches out on one side, whispering, "You look funny. You're not like the others. You're too big, you're too small, you're too tall, you're too short." Vanity and pride reach in from the other side, saying, "Your mom doesn't know what she's talking about—that shirt isn't too tight. Just wear it."

Weeds crowd around our attraction to boys and try to ruin the new blossom. Some of those creeping enemies come through immodest pictures on cell phones, bad texts from friends, movies that make sin look right, or books that want you to grow up too soon. Our world tells us that pouty "sexy" lips are prettier than a friendly smile or that revealing clothes are more attractive than other styles. Don't listen. God's ways are always best.

MOMS: Is there anything in particular you want to encourage or warn your daughter about in this area? Are there any lessons you have learned?

 THE HILL. How could Jesus possibly have anything to do with changing bodies and boys? Talking about him is spiritual talk, and this is girl talk. Can we take a detour past the hill just this once?

Actually, every path we're walking together would be dusty and dry if we didn't pass the lush hill of God's grace. Remember, Jesus didn't just unlock the gate of heaven for us and walk away. He is our most intimate friend, creator, guide, prayer warrior, holy big brother; and his father is our loving father too.

Although Jesus was tempted like we are, he remained pure in every way, and that purity is what makes him so beautiful. It's also what allowed him to die in our place. If he had played in the mud puddles of the world, he couldn't have become the righteous sacrifice we needed.

Purity is beautiful in us too. Walk eagerly and carefully through these growing up years, entrusting yourself fully to God, who likes to surprise his children with joy. Whether in the future you enjoy the gift of marriage or the gift of singleness, you will never regret following the example of your Savior, an example that leads to pure joy.

THE FIELD

- Ask each other how to (and how not to) bring up awkward topics. It's OK to laugh.
- Girls, how can you be an example of purity in your group of friends? It takes courage to change the subject, or not take part in foolish conversations. Moms, how can you be an example of purity to your daughter? Give each other ideas.

- Does your home have appropriate safety measures for wise use of the Internet or other media?
- Moms, pray regularly for and with your daughter during these years. They are challenging and God has given you the privilege of being her cheerleader and guide.

Walk 17
Our Gratitude

Before we head out on today's hike, are you hungry? Let's say I lay before you a banana. It's a nice looking one—yellow and lightly speckled, firm but not mushy. What's your response?

Do you wrinkle your nose and think, *I wish it were a chocolate chip cookie instead . . . or a steaming slice of pepperoni pizza. Come to think of it, even cold pizza would be better than a banana. Why do they always have to go the healthy route? Isn't there anything better around?* By this time your whole face is wrinkled up and you give the banana a disdainful poke, "No thanks."

Or does the banana bring a smile to your face? *Yes, food*, you think, realizing that you hadn't grabbed anything from the pantry before you came. *It's not overripe and I'm starved. I'm so glad there's an extra. All I have left in my backpack is the crust from my lunch sandwich. Now if I can just open it without squishing the end like I always do.*

The two paths of complaining and gratitude lead us to vastly different places, but we often don't realize it until we've hiked a few miles.

THE GARDEN. We serve a God who loves joy, blessing, beauty, singing, celebration, and thanksgiving. Psalms is jammed with calls to worship. Scripture reminds us to rejoice. God made colorful food grow out of the dirt and threw stars in the night sky. He created icebergs and hot springs. He is not a dull God. Sadness and tears do exist in this world, and Psalms speaks of them as well, but God has given us countless blessings. Just think about some of them: the smell of hot chocolate, a refreshing swim, a cozy bed when you're tired, books to read, families to love, and more and more and more.

GIRLS: List out loud as fast as you can fifteen things you're thankful for.

MOMS: List fifteen more. How long did it take you?

Read Ephesians 5:20 and Colossians 3:17.

In these verses, Paul isn't just telling us to fling a quick "thanks" up to the sky; he's telling us to thank *someone*: our generous heavenly Father. Notice that we aren't told to thank him for some things, or the best things, or the easy things; but "whatever we do" we're to thank him "always" for "everything." That's a lot of thanksgiving. Why does God want all that thanks? Does he want to puff himself up? Is he proud and selfish?

No, he isn't. Our thanksgiving does glorify and please and honor God, who is the source of all blessing, but God knows that thanking him will benefit us as well. It reminds us that God is generous and good, that he holds the world in his hands, that we can trust him—and that brings great peace. There is no greater blessing than forgetting about ourselves for a minute and setting our minds on our great God.

MOMS: What percentage of your daily thoughts would you guess include thanksgiving? How often do people hear you expressing thanks? Ask your daughter if you need some help.

GIRLS: What are some things you are often grateful for? What are some things that you should be more grateful for?

THE WEEDS. Who is more fun to be around: grateful people or complaining people? It's hard to be unhappy around a grateful person. They see the good around them, they point out blessings, they feel full and rich from everyday things, and they smile a lot. A complaining person is just the opposite: they notice what's wrong with everything, they think they deserve more than they have, and there is not much that makes them happy. When we started our walk, we talked about how we often don't see where the paths of gratitude or complaining lead until we're a good distance down them. If you find that you're often glum or unhappy or discontented, it's likely you've missed the path of gratitude, and chances are, you're dragging your feet down the path of complaining.

Read Philippians 2:14–15.

When we choose to be thankful rather than complaining, we shine like stars on a dark night. Gratitude is dazzling. People can't help noticing.

It all sounds so easy, doesn't it? But being grateful is not always a breeze; sometimes it's harder work than mowing the lawn or scrubbing a floor. Sometimes it feels like we just can't be grateful. *Life stinks. My friend is mad at me. My hair looks weird. They weren't nice to me. I don't feel like doing my homework. My plans are ruined. I hate broccoli . . .*

BOTH: Describe how you feel when you complain a lot and how you feel when you choose thankfulness. If there is a difference, why?

THE HILL. Here is some incredible news: Jesus has solved your biggest problem, and no, it's not your frizzy hair, your boring math teacher, or the wart on your pinky. Your biggest problem is that your sin has separated you from a holy God, and this is one you have every right to worry and freak out about. This is a problem you should lose sleep over.

Our gracious Savior, Jesus, has solved it, and you didn't have to ask. You didn't deserve it. He chose to love his enemies (that's us) by paying for their sins and inviting them into his family. If you trust in Christ, you are forgiven, rescued, promised a place in heaven, loved, adopted, and cherished by God himself. Now, what were you complaining about again?

The good news of Jesus puts everything in perspective. As we gaze at the mountain of grace in our lives, we can say, "I get to do math!" "I have a table to set!" "I have a friend!" "I have clothes to wear!" When we realize we don't deserve anything, we can be grateful for everything.

We read earlier that the Bible tells us to give thanks in everything. In every circumstance, we see the two paths before us: gratitude and complaining. There is a way to be thankful in every situation, even the hard ones; and there is a way to complain in every situation, even the easy ones.

> **BOTH:** What is difficult in your life right now? What can you give thanks for in that situation?

Let's choose to express gratitude even in the hardest situations. "Thanks for being with me, God." "Thank you that all your promises are true." "Thank you that tomorrow is a new day." These choices to be grateful please the Lord Jesus, and they will keep us on the path that delivers us to that incredible lookout point at the top of the mountain. It's the one with the view of God's glory and splendor, and the one that fills our hearts with inexpressible joy.

 THE FIELD

- **How could you build more thanksgiving into your daily routine? Some ideas to consider: thanking God as soon as you wake up in the morning or as soon as you get into bed at night; creating a "thankful list" for your fridge; or making a bookmark with a thankfulness verse on it.**
- **Who are the people in your life you could express thanks to this week?**
- **Why do you think it is easier to complain than to give thanks?**
- **As mother and daughter, are there ways you can help each other remember to express gratitude, even during difficult times?**
- **End your time together by praying prayers of thanksgiving.**

Walk 18
Our Flair

We're going to break things up a bit today. Instead of a standard walk, we're going to throw some style, some groove, some creativity into it. If I asked you to choose not where, but *how* we're going to walk, what would you say? I'll give you some ideas to jump-start your creativity, then it will be your turn. We could:

- **Run the path in our workout clothes with some energetic tunes pumping in our ears;**
- **Follow the trail without talking much, taking in the surroundings;**
- **Dance down the path with some twirls and leaps and twists;**
- **Meander slowly, sharing our feelings;**
- **Make up silly races and laugh hysterically the whole way;**
- **Find the first good sitting rock and write in our journals or sketch the scene; or**
- **Hike together, stopping to gather pretty wildflowers, leaves, or twigs.**

BOTH: Pick one from the list or make up your own. How would you want to walk?

THE GARDEN. God loves that we each have a different answer to that question. He is the God of thoughtful conversations, silly dances, competitive sprints, and arts and crafts. How do I know? Let's **read 1 Corinthians 12:14–27**. It's a longer (and funnier) passage than usual, so stick with it.

Imagine a body made only of eyes. First of all, that would be creepy, but secondly, it would be sad. How would that person smell or hear or touch anything? If a body only had ears, how would it see? The body of Christ, God's people, works the same way. If we were all artists, who would organize the closets? If we were all quiet thinkers, who would provide the cheerful chitchat? So often we want to be different from the girl or woman God made us to be, and that's both sad and silly. It's like the foot saying, "Boy, I wish I were a nose! I'm tired of being stuck in this shoe all day." But try walking on your nose and you'll see what a bad idea that is. The truth is that our differences reflect God himself because we are made in his image. The poet, the athlete, the dancer, the reader, the organizer, the leader, the joker, and the builder all show something different about the God who made them, and that's an honor.

Let's read 1 Peter 4:10 to see what other use God has for the flair and gifts he's given us.

Did you figure it out? It's to serve one another. You might be thinking that you don't have much to offer, but think again, and remember who made you. The master Designer made you for specific purposes, and there are millions of ways you can brighten the world with your flair.

The best place to start is at home. God loves when we're busy there, making our homes inviting, fun places to be.

Girls, do you like fiddling around in the kitchen? Could you bake cupcakes for the new neighbors or give your mom a break by making spaghetti for dinner?

Are you a go-getter who likes to play sports? Could you entertain the younger neighborhood kids or organize a game night for your own family?

Maybe you've always had a knack for crafts and you have a creative streak. Decorate your house. Arrange a vase of wildflowers for the dinner table. Even pretty weeds can work. Make homemade placemats. Make a bracelet for a new friend, or send a homemade keychain to your grandma.

Maybe you're the quiet thinker type. Could you look for other girls to get in one-on-one conversations with? There are so many people who feel lonely and would love to talk. Could you write a poem to share with your family at dinner or post on the fridge?

These are a few examples of countless ways you can use your flair to serve others and please the Lord.

GIRLS: Name three kinds of activities you enjoy. How could each one be used to "serve one another"?

MOMS: How have you used your unique flair to brighten the lives of those around you?

THE WEEDS. One of the ways sin pollutes the fresh air of God's design is by turning us inward. When we're supposed to be sharing our gifts with others, sin zips us up in a sleeping bag so we can only see the dim, stuffy little world of self.

GIRLS: What is the most claustrophobic, stuffy space you have ever been in? Describe it.

When we're zipped up in selfishness, we become lazy instead of loving others. We point to our own worth instead of God's. We use all our gifts and personality and resources for me, me, me. "How does this affect me?" we ask. "How does this benefit me?" "How can I make myself happier?" "How can I be the star?" But the joke is on us because no joy can penetrate the suffocating air of self-focus, and no one wants to come and join us in there either.

THE HILL. Jesus not only ripped open the zipper of selfishness, but he flung that whole filthy sleeping bag aside. He used his gifts, his personality, and everything he had for others. Jesus enjoyed time with his friends and knew the importance of rest, but Scripture often shows Jesus thinking of others before himself. Instead of relaxing, he healed the sick. Instead of being served, he washed the filthy feet of his disciples. Instead of taking a well-deserved nap, he reached out to an outcast woman. Instead of acting like the king he was, he made breakfast for his disciples. Instead of a fluffy mattress, he often slept on the ground so he could share the good news in different places. Instead of sitting on a royal throne, he suffered on a crude cross. He prayed for people, he comforted people, he encouraged people, he loved people, he taught people, and he gave his very life for people. In doing this, he reflected the wide, loving, sacrificing heart of his Father.

On the cross, Jesus set us free from having to obey our sinful natures. We can breathe the fresh air of self-forgetfulness and service. We can bring joy to the world around us, as well as color and beauty and laughter and thoughtfulness and yumminess and care and conversation and life. And most of the time that brings joy to our own hearts as well. God has so many jobs for us to do and so many ways he wants to use our flair for his kingdom.

Read Ephesians 2:10.

Did you know that God has already prepared ways for you to be a blessing to those around you? Let's give ourselves to Jesus and say, "Use me. I'm yours." He will answer that prayer and show us his will. He will use our words, our magic markers, our songs, our organization, our minds, our crafts, our cupcakes, our hockey games, our homes, and our hands for eternal purposes.

So unzip the sleeping bag. There's a fresh new morning out there.

 THE FIELD

- **Think of one way you can use your flair to brighten your home this week.**
- **Think of one way you can brighten the life of someone outside your family this week.**
- **Consider the different gifts represented in your church and family. How do you see God's wisdom in that? How can understanding 1 Corinthians 12 help us with envy?**
- **In what situation do you feel stuck in that stuffy sleeping bag of self? In what ways can you turn your eyes toward others and breathe the fresh air of love?**
- **Together, ask God to help you see the good works he's prepared for you.**

Walk 19
Our Focus

Today we are going to talk about—hold on a minute, someone is texting me—OK, sorry about that. Today we'll be talking about our focus. So, um—just one second, I want to check one—quick—thing on my phone . . . OK. Thanks. What were we talking about again?

GOD'S DESIGN

The human brain is incredible. It may look like a pile of gray worms in your health book, but it's pretty impressive. If we're at the beach, our brains enable us to simultaneously feel the sand on our feet, taste the salty water on our lips, hear the seagulls cackling, smell the boardwalk fries, and examine a clamshell. Then it yawns and waits for a real challenge.

God made our minds with mental muscle so we could know him, consider his great works, and enjoy his creation. Our minds are constantly on the go, but with so many topics to think about, how can they stay on course?

Philippians 4:8 lists the kinds of thoughts we are to think. How many are there?

Let's give this a test run. What could we think about that falls into these categories? We could think about friendship, how interesting our world is, how to respond humbly to an insult, or how much fun vacation is going to be. We could figure out the best solution to a problem we're having, and we could certainly practice our math. We would probably have to stop thinking about the gossip we heard and the dumb show we watched last night—and how unfair it is that our sister got out of table-clearing duty. God wants our minds to dwell on what is good and pleasing to him.

MOMS: List out loud the topics you've thought about within the last few hours. (Be honest.) How many of them fit into the categories in Philippians 4:8?

GIRLS: Do the same thing. List at least four things you've thought about and give them the Philippians test.

I wonder why Paul gave his readers those instructions. Did he think his readers wouldn't fill their minds with the right things? Did he think they'd get distracted?

THE WEEDS. I wonder if Paul would have wanted a cell phone. It would have been much easier to text or e-mail his letter to the church in Philippi instead of writing it out with a pen, and maybe he even could have FaceTimed them. Better yet, he could have taken a selfie when he met the high priest. Poor Paul. He missed all those opportunities.

All our neat devices help us in countless ways, but they're tricky too. They can distract us from what we should be doing and from what is true and pure and lovely. So do we go back to *Little House on the Prairie* days and unplug completely? No way! But let's know what to watch for.

Say your dad comes home from work, throws his bag on a chair, and says, "Tell me about your day, honey." But you noticed his phone slip out of his bag, and you've been trying to beat your high score on a game all week. You reach for it (or your own phone if you have one) automatically. "It was OK," you answer as your eyes follow the figure on the screen and your fingers start dancing. He says something else but wanders away in a minute and you're free to play.

Was that sin? Probably not. Was playing the game a better choice than talking with your dad? Probably not. Did your game end up being praiseworthy and excellent? Probably not. Games and entertainment are gifts from God that can refresh us, but watch them. They can distract us and suck the life from what's most important.

GIRLS: What is your favorite phone or computer game right now?

MOMS: What is your biggest distraction on your electronic devices?

The very first two verses of Psalm 1 tell us what a person the Lord considers "blessed" thinks about. **Read Psalm 1:1–2** and look for what this person delights in and meditates on.

So you roll out of bed, grab your devotional and fuzzy blanket, and curl up in the corner chair. You are going to meditate on God's Word! The devotional directs you to a passage in Proverbs and you use the Bible app on your device. Halfway through reading the passage, a text pops up from your friend about a homework assignment. You answer her quickly and get back to work but then think of the perfect remark to send back to her. In a few minutes, you've completely lost your focus. Proverbs was a little bit confusing anyway, and some of the words seemed a little old-fashioned. Maybe you'll pick it up again tomorrow.

What happened here is common to all of us. When given the chance, we will usually choose an easier task over a harder one.

Sending a text to a friend is easier than studying the Bible, but it will not bring the blessing God promises.

Technology isn't the only distraction in life, but it is a massive one. It's easier to watch YouTube videos than read a book. It's easier to text funny comments than have a meaningful conversation. It's easier to play a game than memorize Scripture. It's easier to look at social media than study for a test. Some of us may get so used to distractions that we forget how to sit down and concentrate on anything.

MOMS: Do you find that your attention span has increased or decreased in the past five years?

GIRLS: What "harder task" would you like to accomplish even though it will take some focus?

THE HILL. Part of the reason people today are so distracted is that they're looking for joy. We all are. God has placed that desire inside us and the good news is that Jesus offers us a joy that outshines any other. Watching a funny video can be entertaining, like tossing a stone in a puddle and watching the splash. There's nothing wrong with that. But meditating on God is like diving into the clear Caribbean and exploring a coral reef. There is no end to the wonders you will find. Enjoy the fun that flies into your life, but don't let the distractions keep you in the puddles when there are oceans to explore.

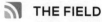 **THE FIELD**

- A list of priorities can help keep us on track as we dodge the distractions that fly at us. Try listing your top five priorities now. If you need some help, here are some ideas that you can rearrange together:
  - Loving God (prayer, Bible reading, obedience)
  - Loving my family
  - Serving the church
  - Pursuing good friendships
  - Reaching out to others
  - Being faithful in schoolwork
  - Entertainment and relaxation
- Spend a day without any media (TV, phone, computer, etc.) and see if you notice any differences in your lives.
- Are there any guidelines or rules that would help you to avoid distraction? Should phones be docked while at home? Should computer games only be played at certain times? Should Mom and Dad lead by example in some way?
- How could the two of you grow in delighting "in the law of the Lᴏʀᴅ" and meditating on it day and night?

Walk 20
Our Fear

After hearing today's title, you might wonder if we'll be trekking through gloomy, bat-infested caverns slick with dripping water, where our darkest fears will float out and touch us as we pass. I'm happy to tell you there are no cave explorations today, but hang onto your flashlights because we will be peering into shadowy corners of our hearts.

Sometimes fears are healthy. We fear hornets because they can sting. Only a fool would boast, "I'm not scared," and stick her hand into a hornet's nest. But sometimes fears are ridiculous, and our imaginations puff them up until they're the size of three-story floats in the Thanksgiving Day parade.

MOMS: Name two of your fears: one healthy and one ridiculous.

GIRLS: Your turn. Share the two fears that came to mind for you.

🌻 **THE GARDEN.** On our walk today we'll be looking for healthy fears and unhealthy fears. Gardens don't seem particularly scary, especially the Garden of Eden where you wouldn't fear anything, not even tigers. Imagine rubbing their bellies and hearing them purr.

God had set his people in perfect surroundings, but he also told them something.

Read Genesis 2:15–17.

Yikes. The phrase "surely die" doesn't seem to fit with the puffy clouds and gurgling brooks of Eden. It appears that God thought a certain kind of fear did belong in his perfect place—a healthy fear of God himself.

Just to make sure, take a look at **Deuteronomy 10:12**.

The first thing God wants is for us to fear him. This isn't the kind of fear that runs away screaming; it's the kind that respects, stands in awe, wants to please, and dreads disobeying. God is good and loving, but he is also our creator and master, and far beyond our imaginations. The psalmist says, "He lifts his voice, the earth melts" (Psalm 46:6 NIV). That's a power worthy of fear.

> **MOMS:** Do you remember a specific time when you felt the vast power of God and it scared you?

✳ **THE WEEDS.** Adam and Eve probably knew God's voice could melt the earth; after all, he spoke it into existence. But they chucked their healthy fear of God into the trash when they ate the forbidden fruit; we aren't much wiser. Instead of fearing God and living to please him, we often end up fearing other people and living to please them, even though their voices can't melt an M&M. The Bible calls this "fear of man," and it's living upside-down. It doesn't make sense that we worry more about pleasing people than about pleasing the Almighty, but it's so natural. Have you ever felt it? If you've ever been distracted by what someone thought of you, you've felt it. If you've ever felt self-conscious about what you were wearing, tried hard to be the center of attention, compared yourself with someone else, or been tempted not to answer a question truthfully, you've felt it. We all have.

Read Proverbs 29:25.

GIRLS: Have you ever seen or read about a snare in a movie or book? What was it like and what was it catching?

A snare is a trap. It fools us, hooks us, and hurts us in the end. But it's tricky. Fear of man is often camouflaged as something else. If we don't look closely, we won't even know it's there. Making people happy is good, right? We want people to like us. We want to feel self-confident. We want to be thought of as nice.

Of course we do! But how much do we want those things? Do we want to be liked so much that we'll join in with a group of friends who are mocking someone? Do we want to be the nice girl so much that we tell people what they want to hear instead of the truth? Do we fear the opinions of others so much that we won't stand up for what is right or reach out to an unpopular kid? Do we worship others' opinions so much that one small criticism sticks with us for days and years? Fear of man may be camouflaged, but when you know what you're looking for, you see it everywhere. It snares everyone.

GIRLS: Now that you know a little more about it, where do you see fear of man lurking in your life?

MOMS: When are you most tempted to fear man, and how do you handle that?

THE HILL. How can we stop caring so much about what others think? Other people surround us—they're everywhere. We hear their comments, sense their gaze, and long for their acceptance. Only a fool would say their opinions don't matter. And they do matter. They matter like a flickering candle. God matters like the blazing sun.

The way we grow in a healthy fear of God is by learning about him and talking to him. God knew we could never approach him because he is holy, so he sacrificed his own son to bring us to himself—and Jesus was a willing sacrifice. When we see his holiness, and mercy, and the extreme price he paid for us, his thoughts begin to matter more and more. Gradually, our friend's disapproval or the party we weren't invited to don't matter quite so much anymore.

We learn to laugh at ourselves, forgive offenses, and worry less about what others think. We become freer and happier and find ourselves wanting to please God more than everyone around us. The temptations won't go away, and people's opinions do matter, but their chains have fallen off because we belong to Jesus.

The same truth applies to all our fears, even very real ones. Do you fear the dark? Do you fear an angry relative? Do you fear doing badly in school? Do you fear spiders? Those are all real fears and they matter. But Psalm 56:3–4 says: "When I am afraid, I put my trust in you. In God, whose word I praise, in God I trust; I shall not be afraid. What can flesh do to me?"

"Flesh" just means people and the world around us. What can they really do to me when I have God? Memorize that line, "When I am afraid, I put my trust in you," and pray it aloud when you hear fear knocking.

THE FIELD

- On a scale from one to ten, how would you each rank your "fear of God" and your "fear of man"?
- Who specifically do you fear more than God? A particular friend? A teacher?
- After what situations do you find yourself worrying about how you did or what others thought of you?
- Pray together right now and ask God to help you both grow in the fear of him.

Before we head out on the path today, we're going to change into some walking clothes. Yours will be a moth-eaten house dress from your great-grandma's attic trunk. Ready? Let's go.

Wait. You don't like the outfit? You're not in a hurry to go out in public wearing it? Why are you hiding?

The reason you would be hiding if you really had to wear that outfit is because our clothes make a statement about us. They say something about who we are. Though worn on the outside, they reflect the inside. Let's say someone gave you and a random group of girls your age each $30 and dropped you off at a clothing store you agreed on. When you met at the checkout, one of you might have a purple T-shirt with a bright yellow flower on it, one might have leopard-print pants, one might have a sleeveless black dress, and one might have striped footy pajamas. Each of those items would say a little something about the girl holding it, and that makes life fun.

GIRLS: If we went shopping right now, what store would you go to, and what item would you buy?

MOMS: Looking back, what was the ugliest outfit you ever wore?

THE GARDEN. God created variety, beauty, color, style, and creativity. He designed the leopard's print. He made us to show off his glory, and we can do that not only with our words and actions, but with our wardrobes. Yes, God even cares about our closets.

Read Proverbs 31:22 to find out what a famous godly woman wore.

"Fine linen and purple" might not be what all the girls in the neighborhood are wearing now, but in those days, they were the talk of the town. This woman was well dressed. Now read verse 30 of the very same chapter.

This woman is honored for dressing nicely, yet we are reminded that beauty is fleeting. Attractive clothes may be a good thing, but there are qualities that are much more important. Let's see what else God has to say about our clothes.

Look at 1 Timothy 2:9–10.

Before you unbraid your hair and chuck your mom's gold hoop earrings in the trash, let's examine this. God wants us to dress respectably, in a way that's appropriate for the situation. He also wants us to dress with modesty and self-control. These words might seem vague. What is respectful dress? What do modesty and self-control look like for us? God hasn't included a clothing catalog in the Bible, but he's given us consciences that usually know when we are dressing to show off; and just as importantly, he's given us moms to help us figure these things out.

THE WEEDS. Paul had some concerns about the girls in Timothy's church. (He had some concerns about the guys too, but we'll leave that for them.) In those days, some women were spending hours braiding their hair into complicated designs. It was considered "showy" in their culture, and it took hours to do. These verses aren't telling us never to braid our hair, they're saying, "Listen girls, don't *just* spend your time on physical beauty. Don't obsess over your hair and clothes and accessories. Think about your inner beauty and let your outward beauty be secondary." A kind heart and loving actions are what God considers absolutely stunning.

MOMS: Do you notice any of the weeds that Paul saw around you? They could be in stores, in the media, or in your own closets. (These weeds include disrespectful or inappropriate clothing, immodesty, or too much time spent on dress.)

Some girls think modesty means wearing big, ugly clothes; the bigger and uglier, the better. The godliest woman in the world must be wearing a giant burlap bag that still smells of old potatoes! But that's not what modesty means. It's a silly stereotype that's almost ruined the word for us.

GIRLS: What do you think the word *modesty* really means?

If you said something about being humble, you were right. It means not thinking of yourself too highly; not drawing too much attention to yourself; not living in a way that shouts, "Look at me. I'm the richest or prettiest or craziest girl around." It also means not showing off too much of your body and looking for attention that way. As Christians, we want to point to God's greatness, not our own. We want him to be the star of the show. Jesus was the model of modesty, using every opportunity to point to his Father.

So we can be modest in speech by not always trying to be the loudest and silliest all the time. We can be modest in our actions by not trying to be noticed for every good deed we do. We can be modest in dress by wearing clothes that are fun and stylish but don't draw unnecessary attention to ourselves, that don't reveal too much of our bodies.

Ever since sin entered the world, our hearts don't naturally focus on God—or others. Our thoughts are often more centered on ourselves. We may find ourselves more interested in being admired than exercising modesty or self-control; more interested in popularity than humility; more interested in good accessories than good works!

MOMS: When are you tempted to think more about what you're wearing than how you're acting?

GIRLS: Do you feel pressure from your friends to wear the right clothes or wear clothes that make you look older?

THE HILL. Let's look at one last passage in the Bible that talks about clothes, and this time it's not about ours. **Read John 20:3–9.**

Can you imagine the risen Jesus, carefully folding up the burial cloth that had been around his head? But he wasn't just folding up linen, he was folding up death. He folded up Satan's plans for us, laid them in a corner, and left them in the tomb. Then he stepped out into the sunlight and ushered in new life for all of us: a life where sins had been paid for, Satan had been defeated, heaven had been opened, and God and people could be brought together.

Because Jesus folded the burial cloth and conquered death for us, we know that God loves us and accepts us. Because of that, our clothes can be attractive, but they don't have to show us off, or get us attention, or reveal too much. We're cherished and valued by God. Best of all, we can stop thinking of ourselves all the time. We have someone better to think about. If we're not wearing the latest styles or getting the most attention, it's really not that important. Our new shoes will scuff and fade; God's love won't.

 THE FIELD

- **Does the word** *modesty* **sound silly or old-fashioned to you? What does it mean to you?**
- **Growing bigger every year makes this difficult, but are there particular clothes in your closet that might be too tight or too revealing?**
- **Can each of you think of a person you think dresses stylishly but respectfully? Maybe you can get some tips from her about where and how she shops.**
- **What is a specific way you can pursue modesty in your words? Your actions? Your clothes?**

Walk 22
Our Reach

Nobody likes being lost. When I realize I've made a wrong turn on a busy highway, the PANIC button gets pushed in my mind and a red light starts blinking on my forehead. "Shut down immediately!" it commands my brain. "Change all clear thought to total confusion! Blur the vision. Rev up the heart!" A friend of mine has a different response. If he makes a wrong turn, he (not the car) starts to overheat and he opens the windows as fast as he can, even if it's freezing outside.

> **GIRLS:** What do your parents do when they make a wrong turn on the highway or realize they're lost?

Sometimes we're lost and we don't know it, and that takes us even further in the wrong direction. Have you ever been walking through a crowded area with your family and realized in horror after several minutes that they were nowhere in sight? You may have been whistling a tune while you strolled, but the truth is you were lost.

> **MOMS:** Describe a time you got really lost, and maybe didn't realize it for a while.

THE GARDEN. We've walked together many times through the garden, beside the weeds, past the hill, and into the field. Our trail map, the Bible, has kept us on course, but did you know there are a lot of lost people wandering around on other paths? Most of them are whistling a tune and don't even know they need directions. They've never seen the hill or understood what Jesus has done for them, and even if they have glimpsed it from a distance, they haven't trusted in Jesus for forgiveness.

GIRLS: How often do you think about the fact that people around you don't know Jesus? Are there times you're more or less aware of it?

Jesus was a busy man, but he never forgot his purpose. In Luke, he tells a story that shows us his heart for the lost.

Read Luke 15:3–7.

Losing one sheep doesn't seem like a big deal to us, but to a shepherd, it would have been a huge problem. A shepherd's job was to take care of the sheep and keep them safe. Jesus knows that if a shepherd lost a sheep, he would go into the open country and do whatever was necessary to find it. When he found it, the shepherd would carry it to safety on his shoulders.

Jesus is that shepherd who risked everything and went in search of us. If we're Christians, then we were once lost sheep, which were placed on the shoulders of our great shepherd. God's desire is that we would have that same shepherd's heart for others. He wants us to love and go after lost sheep, remembering that we were once lost ourselves.

✳ **THE WEEDS.** This story shows us the loving, fatherly heart of the Lord, but its message can sometimes offend people. Some would say that it's rude or proud to claim there is a right way to God or that people might be on the wrong path. They might think there are many ways to God, and we shouldn't judge someone else's choice. We certainly want to be loving and humble toward others, but we can't forget the clear truth Jesus spoke in John 14:6.

He is the way to the Father—not *a* way, but *the* way. There is one path to the joy of heaven, and it's he. Because of this, it's crazy for us to find the right path without helping others do the same, but it takes courage to be a shepherd. It takes courage to leave the familiar company of the other sheep and go find that lost one. It takes courage to share the good news of Jesus with others. We don't know how they'll respond. They might think we're strange or call us old-fashioned. Sharing the gospel is risky business. The direction our culture is moving will require us to have even more courage to share our faith. But if we love others, sharing our joy with them is worth any risk.

> **GIRLS:** What are some of the risks you are aware of when you think about sharing the gospel with others?
>
> **MOMS:** Do you think there are specific challenges in our culture that make it especially difficult to share that Jesus is the only way to God?

🔺 **THE HILL.** The unique aspect of the shepherd story is that it's not just a story; Jesus lived it. A few chapters later in Luke, Jesus enters Jerusalem and the good shepherd really does lay down his life for the sheep by dying for us. His example of sacrifice and love shows us how to love others. The religious leaders of his time self-righteously stuck their noses in the air and condemned people, but Jesus wasn't like that. He loved people no matter who they were. He saw value in them and showed them the way.

Do you remember, in the parable, how the shepherd and his friends rejoiced when that lost sheep was brought home? That's how Jesus rejoiced when he rescued us, and that's the kind of joy we will ultimately experience when we share the good news with others. When we come alongside people in love and share how God has rescued us, we are following in the footsteps of our great Shepherd.

THE FIELD

- **Who are the people closest to you who don't know the Lord? Have you had an opportunity to share the gospel with them?**
- **Do you know someone who very naturally shares their faith? What can you learn from him or her?**
- **If this is an area of weakness for you, the Holy Spirit is happy to help you. We always need his power to obey. Ask him to show you specific opportunities where you could invite someone to church or reach out to someone.**
- **If someone asked you why you go to church or what it means to be a Christian, what would you say?**

Walk 23
Our Doubts

Our minds are question factories. They crank out little questions, medium-sized questions, and huge questions all day long. Sticking our head in the fridge and yelling, "What can I eat?" is a little question. Doing homework and wondering, *What am I going to be when I grow up?* is a medium-sized question. Staring at the Big Dipper and whispering, "Does anybody up there really know me?" is a cosmic, epic, gigantic, galactic question. It's a big question. It's a question that sometimes even crashes into the heads of those who love the Lord.

We have eyes and we're used to seeing things. We see our friends, we see our beds, we see our grilled cheese sandwiches, we see the teeny ant crawling across the page we're trying to read. If we can't see, then we hear. We hear the raindrops on our windowpane at night, the fire engine siren, our dad calling our name. If we don't see *or* hear something, then maybe we smell: frying bacon, spring mulch, stinky socks. You get the idea. We're used to sensing proof that something exists.

But we cannot see, hear, smell, taste, or feel God. Yet.

GIRLS: Do you ever wish you could see God? Where would you like to meet him? How do you think you would react?

 **THE GARDEN**

Read Hebrews 11:6.

We need faith to believe that God is real, and all he says he is in his Word. God isn't a fairy-tale prince, and he doesn't expect us to squeeze our eyes shut, breathe in some pixie dust, and believe in him. He's given us every reason in the world to trust him, and at the top of that list is his creation, his Word, and his Son.

God built a world that sings his name. Signs of his handiwork surround us, but we get so used to them that we can't see what's in front of us. After a tough day, we might ask, "Is there really a God?" The words come out between mouthfuls of a juicy peach that grew on a tree that magically emerged from the ground, which is in the shape of a giant ball called Earth that rotates around a glowing star that gives us precise amounts of heat and light. This world has its Designer's signature written all over it, and each crashing wave, newborn baby, and distant galaxy is meant to remind us of him.

Read about how creation speaks to us in **Romans 1:19–21**.

> **MOMS:** What part of creation encourages your own faith the most?

God didn't stop with creation, he gave us the Bible: a book full of words breathed out by God himself. Through these inspired words, God leads us, encourages us, and most importantly, tells us the story of his amazing grace to sinners. Psalms describes the Bible as "a lamp to my feet and a light to my path" (Psalm 119:105).

What a perfect description of a book that shows us which way to go and provides hope in dark times.

> **GIRLS:** Do you remember a time when you were walking through the dark with a flashlight? How did that light make you feel? Why do you think God's Word is described that way?

✳ **THE WEEDS.** God has given us minds that want to understand things. That's why inventors invent, scientists experiment, and astronomers study the sky. God is not afraid of our questions, even when they're about him. He's designed our minds to ask them, and he's big enough to answer. Some questions will be answered by parents or pastors or life experience. Other questions will only be answered in heaven. Questions aren't anything to worry about, but we need to start paying more attention to them when they turn into doubts about God. Doubts suggest that God is not who he says he is. "Maybe God's not good. Maybe he doesn't know what he's doing. Maybe he doesn't exist at all." A thoughtful question like, "Why does God allow pain in this world?" can turn into doubt that decides, "He must not be loving."

I have a vegetable garden, and I usually tend it pretty well until July when I start to get tired of it. I get tired of bending over and pulling weeds and fighting insects, so I ignore it. When I finally tromp out there to pick a tomato or two, sometimes the weeds are so tall I can barely see the smaller plants. Even though the plants are real, and are even bearing fruit, they look like they don't exist. If I don't deal with those weeds, they choke out my green beans and lettuce in no time.

Doubts are a little bit like those weeds. They can grow tall quickly and overshadow the little plant of faith that is growing and bearing fruit in our hearts. If we don't deal with them, they can gradually choke the life right out of our faith.

> **BOTH:** What are some of the hardest questions that you've wondered about? Have any of them turned into doubts about God?

THE HILL. God's creation and his Word are huge helps to our wavering faith, but God went even further. He decided to show himself to us. He sent his Son into the world so human beings could see him with their own eyes. Those people recorded what Jesus did, and now we can "see" Jesus through Scripture. Did you know that Jesus is the exact picture of God?

Read Hebrews 1:1–6.

Do you want to know what God is like? Look at Jesus. See him instruct his disciples. See him welcome the children being sent away. See him reach out to the sinful woman at the well. See him willingly dying on the cross for us. That's a picture of God who loves you so much. He instructs you, he welcomes you, he wants to talk to you, and he even died for you.

Don't let your hard questions scare you. But if those questions start turning into big, bad doubts, first, open your eyes to creation. Ask yourself who designed the intricate world around you and your own extraordinary body. Second, read the Bible. The truths it holds will strengthen your faith. Ask your parents or pastor for help in finding the answers you need. Third, look to Jesus. His eyes see you, his ears hear your prayers, his hands bear the scars that show you his love. You will find that God not only exists, but that he, like Hebrews 11:6 says, "rewards those who seek him."

 THE FIELD

- We get so used to the world God has given us. What are some things in nature that show that someone designed it, and it didn't just come into existence by chance?
- What questions about God do you have? Though mysteries remain, how could the two of you pursue answers?
- If you had to describe Jesus to someone from what you know of him in the Bible, how would you describe him? Try it, and remember that he is the exact picture of God.
- How do you think God might "reward those who seek him"?

" It's time to clean your room," Dad announces on a perfectly good Saturday morning.

The dreaded words have been spoken. Misery descends like a fog. Birds stop chirping. Bees stop buzzing. The world awaits your response.

"OK," you reply in a weak voice, picturing the floor of your room, or what used to be the floor before the dirty clothes covered it. You force your feet down the hall to your room and the monstrous task begins.

I admit that's a tad dramatic, but it might not be far from the truth. Even if we're the organized type, our rooms can take on a life of their own. What is it, really, that makes cleaning them so unpleasant? Is it the vacuum cleaner or the dust spray? No, it's the stuff. The stuff that mysteriously multiplies daily. The stuff that scatters itself on our floors, that wiggles its way under our beds, and that piles itself onto our dressers.

Our lives involve a lot of stuff. We have stuff for school and stuff for sports; stuff for crafts and stuff for accessorizing; stuff for winter and stuff for summer. We can buy things to help carry our stuff, sort our stuff, store our stuff, and clean our stuff. When we travel, we even need suitcases to take our stuff with us.

> **GIRLS:** If your house was burning down and you could grab only five possessions, what would you grab?
>
> **MOMS:** How about you? (Assume all family members are safe.)

THE GARDEN. Our possessions show how generous God has been to us. Think of the things you love: movies, pets, games, snacks, your favorite T-shirt. Each of those items can remind you how kind God is.

Read James 1:17.

God loves that we enjoy the world he created for us, and he loves to provide for our needs. We can even use those gifts for his kingdom. At times, we can wrongly picture holiness as a hermit reading his Bible on a hard wooden chair in his cave, but would you want to go over to that guy's house for dinner? You might have raw fish and a hunk of stale bread. The things we own can show cheer and care and beauty. It's nice to have fun plates to serve snacks on or an extra pair of roller blades to share when friends come over. People love to see us in a new dress for Easter, even if it's from the second-hand store. Our stuff isn't bad, it's a blessing, and we should thank God for it. But like the forty-one mismatched socks in our dresser drawer, our stuff can begin to tangle us up.

THE WEEDS. Do you know what the first of the Ten Commandments is? God said, "You shall have no other gods before me" (Exodus 20:3). You don't have any little Baal statues or voodoo dolls sitting on your windowsill, so you might think that's the easiest commandment to obey. But actually, false gods don't have to be statues. They can be anything that replaces the true God in our lives, anything we love more than him. A false god can be a band that we love, a best friend, a feeling of comfort, or a sense of control if it replaces God in importance. False gods can also be—you guessed it—our stuff.

As usual, sin wants to take the gifts and blessings we've received from God and turn them against him, so that we love the gift more than the giver. We need to enjoy all that God has given us but remember where our real treasure is.

The Bible says a lot about stuff and treasure. **Read Matthew 6:19–21** and decide what you think the last sentence means.

God gives us a sneak peek into what will matter in the end. It's like knowing the answers to a test ahead of time. He says, "Listen, I know the things on earth seem irresistible, but they really won't last. Value the things I love and obey me. Then lasting treasure will be stored up for you."

GIRLS: Have you ever seen a dump or a junkyard? Describe it. How do you think the items you named in the previous question will look in two hundred years?

MOMS: Describe something of yours that moths and rust (or time) have destroyed.

Stuff doesn't last, but loving God does. Reaching out to a lonely person is storing up treasure. Filling up your dad's water glass is storing up treasure. Sweeping the walk without being asked or encouraging someone is storing up treasure. Those are the kinds of treasure that will never fade.

Here's the challenge: An incredible amount of money is spent in our country each year to convince you that earthly treasure will bring lasting joy. Your brain is receiving messages everywhere you go that say, "If you buy this shirt, you will dazzle strangers on the street." "If you watch this movie, you'll be laughing hysterically with your popular friends." "If you buy this phone, you'll finally be like all the other kids and be accepted." Once we get one product, we realize we need a different one, or more of them, or the latest version, or the one our friend has, or the one from the other store.

They are all lies.

The products are nice and you'll enjoy them. Clothes and movies and phones are wonderful, and buying them can be loads of fun. But the joy they bring is like a lollipop. It's sweet for a while but then melts away to nothing. Lots of grown-ups try to fill their longing for joy by shopping and spending more than they should. It brings them temporary happiness, and when that fades they have to go out and do it again.

MOMS: Have you ever used shopping for something new as a way to fill a deeper longing?

GIRLS: What item is the media currently trying to sell you?

THE HILL. God wants to fill us up with his Spirit. Jesus died and rose so he could send the Holy Spirit to live in our hearts. We don't have to fill our empty hearts with stuff. He wants to fill our hearts. He doesn't want us to waste our energies and investments on things that will be in a dump someday. He wants us to invest in treasure that won't rust, or fade, or shrink, or be out of style in a year.

So what do we do? Go find a cave next to that hermit we talked about earlier? Nope; go shopping, buy the things you need, enjoy the gifts God has given, delight in his creativity, laugh with your mom in the dressing room, look for great sales. But do all of these things rejoicing that your Father is the giver of all good gifts, and that he keeps your real treasure in heaven.

Invest in what lasts. Serve, give, share, worship, pray, love, apologize, encourage. And don't worry when you spill grape juice on your favorite shirt. It was going to fade anyway.

THE FIELD

- Ask each other if you value your possessions too highly. Clues will be how you react when things get ruined, how quick you are to share, and how content you are with what you have.
- What kinds of products does the media convince you that you must have? Clothes? Items for the home? Entertainment? Food?
- What is one way that each of you can show that you want to invest in heavenly treasure this week? Some suggestions are sharing a prized possession with someone or serving someone in a way you usually wouldn't.
- Begin to discuss marketing techniques as you see them. When commercials come on or you drive by billboards, talk about what they are trying to convince you of—and then remind each other of the truth.

Walk 25
Our Hard Times

Depending on where you live, you may have seen a boardwalk. They are wooden walkways built along the beach, usually lined with pizza shops and about a thousand stores selling hermit crabs and T-shirts.

MOMS: What's your favorite boardwalk memory?

Everybody knows you shouldn't step onto the boardwalk barefoot, but everybody does it anyway. One day, I was walking the boards, following my nose to a pizza stand, when I got the splinter of my life. Surely an entire two-by-four was sticking out of my foot. As I hobbled to a sun-beaten bench, my dream of steaming pizza was replaced by a cloud of gloom. *I may never survive this! I may never walk again! Look at all those other barefoot rebels carrying their pizzas, free of a harpoon in their foot. Why me? Why now? I hate this place.*

Sound familiar? Were you ever trekking along in life, carefree and content, when, "Bam!" a trial dropped out of the sky (or popped out of the ground) and benched you? If you haven't, you will, and it's important to know what to think while we're stuck on that bench watching the world, and their pizzas, go by.

GIRLS: Describe the worst splinter you ever got? Who is the best splinter-getter-outer in your family?

THE GARDEN. In the Garden of Eden, life was bliss; there were no bad days. That didn't last long though because Adam and Eve snorted at God's commands, tasted the fruit, and regretted it for the rest of their lives. The trials they experienced as God disciplined them and cast them out of the garden were a result of their own foolishness. We might think that hard times have no purpose since they weren't part of God's original design. But here comes that baffling grace again: our holy God is also redemptive. That means he takes what is ruined and makes it beautiful. Even our worst times can be used for glorious purposes.

Read James 1:2–4.

Count it all what? Joy? I counted that splinter a curse, a bother, a pain, a wretched interruption in my peaceful day. How could there be joy in the trial when it seemed like the trial had stolen my joy and fed it to the seagulls? And why does that verse say "when" you meet trial? Wouldn't "if" be better? That way we could step very carefully and avoid them.

The reality is that because of sin, this world is broken and full of trials. No careful stepping will keep us from them. We've all experienced the smaller problems: skinned knees, lost homework, an argument. But maybe you have had the whopper trials too. How would we count them joy? How would we count divorced parents joy, or the death of a loved one? How about a difficult family situation, loud arguments, rejection, friendlessness, sickness? Should we count them joy?

The joy James writes about isn't a celebrating, jumping up and down kind of joy. It's a deeper, peaceful joy that comes from knowing that God uses trials to mature us and has glorious purposes we will someday understand. Hard times build steadfastness—they teach us to trust God and endure. That kind of maturity pleases God and shapes us into the people he wants us to be.

But God loves us as he shapes us. Do you remember the story of how Jesus raised Lazarus from the dead (John 11)? Jesus wept with Mary and Martha outside the tomb of their brother, Lazarus. He knew Lazarus would come back to life and it would all be fixed, but still he cried. He cries with us too. He comforts us. He puts his arms around us. We can trust that while these hard times last, God will draw us close to himself, use them for our good, and show us a joy—yes, joy—deeper than the world knows, that comes from trusting him in the darkest days.

MOMS: What is one of the hardest trials you have endured? What did God show you through it?

GIRLS: What trials—small, medium, or large—are you facing right now?

When I was nine, my dad died of cancer. That's a bigger deal than the boardwalk splinter. But guess what? It didn't derail God. Because in his sovereignty he rules all things, he allowed it to happen and he redeemed it. If you're his child, that same loving God rules your life too. He is working through the hard things in your life to build a steadfast woman who trusts him, and you can be certain he will show himself faithful.

Girls, as we apply these truths, let's remember that God has given us parents so we don't walk the path alone. They want to guide and encourage us, but they can't if we aren't open with them. Tell them everything—feelings, fears, things you feel weird about, temptations, hurts. Chances are, they've had similar experiences, and they can help you and pray for you.

✳ **THE WEEDS.** Remember the way the serpent tempted Eve in the garden? He said, "You don't really believe what God said, do you?" When we go through dark valleys, it's easy to forget God's promises and feel like he doesn't care or isn't in control. If we believe those lies, then there's only one thing left to do: take matters into our own hands. So we worry, fret, fear, scheme, pout, and freak out. That never helps much, does it?

> **GIRLS:** Which reaction in the sentence above is closest to what you do when bad things happen? Can you think of an example?

I've done them all. The weeds wind around my ankles and keep me stuck in that hopeless place. Then I finally look up and see the hill.

🌄 **THE HILL.** The hill is the answer to everything. No weed is strong enough to climb it. The empty cross and empty tomb remind us that Jesus paid for our sins so we could be part of God's family. When we become Christians by trusting him, God becomes our Father and promises to use all our hard times for our good and his glory.

Read Romans 8:28. You may want to memorize this promise so you can pull it out whenever you need it. It's a good weed killer.

"ALL things work together for good." That includes bullying, a broken arm, moving across the country, and even silly things like losing your favorite earrings. All things. The hard times will still be hard. The messed up world will still be messed up. But knowing that our heavenly Father controls all things and promises to turn even the nastiest problems into something good should bring a deep peace to our hearts. That peace can sometimes be hard to find, but once again we have our map to give us directions.

Read Philippians 4:6–7.

Try to figure out what we are supposed to do when we are anxious, and what God will do in response.

When we're feeling anxious, we aren't supposed to fret and freak out, we are to come to our Father, tell him our needs, and thank him for who he is. And he will give us peace—more than we can imagine—and stand guard at the door of our hearts and minds.

Life can be messy, but in Jesus there is joy and peace even in the mess. No trial is too small for him to notice. No trial is too big for him to handle. Bring them before your Father. He will redeem each one.

 THE FIELD

- **Name one trial that God has used for good in your life, then try to say Romans 8:28 from memory.**
- **In what area can each of you begin to follow the instructions in Philippians 4:6–7?**
- **Pray for each other, asking that God would help you to consider your trials "pure joy."**
- **Do you know someone who is going through a hard time? Write them a note now, reminding them of the verses you looked at today. Encourage them that God is with them and will work all things for good.**

We've done it! We've taken twenty-five walks together, admiring the gardens, stomping through weeds, gazing at the hill, and working in the field. If you didn't skip anything, you've studied around eighty Scripture passages and talked yourselves through over two hundred discussion questions. Those walks have made us stronger in our relationships with God and with each other. Exercise pays off, even when it's mostly our minds and mouths doing the workout.

GIRLS: Which walk did you like best?

MOMS: Which walk did you find most helpful to the two of you?

🌹 **THE GARDEN.** If we could all get together and take a real, live walk today, I'd have us climb a mountain—a serious one like Everest or the Matterhorn. We'd have to link up first because one of the greatest dangers climbers face when crossing glaciers are giant cracks in the ice called crevasses. They can be hundreds of feet deep, but the scariest part is that climbers can't see them because they are covered with snow. Imagine walking along and suddenly the snow beneath you caves in and you hurtle into a deep pit, your heart frozen in fear. Then suddenly you stop. Dangling by a rope with a dark chasm beneath you, you realize that the teammates you were roped to have grabbed the ice with their picks and stopped you. After being hauled up, you collapse on the snow, never so happy to see the sun. If a lone climber falls into a crevasse they will die, and many have. Climbers need to stay together to summit, and so do we.

Read Ecclesiastes 4:9–10.

Here we see the same point: we can't go it alone. Life has pitfalls and we need to walk with others. Right now, an important person you should be linked to is your mom. Even though mother-daughter relationships can have their rough spots, walking together brings protection and blessing.

> **GIRLS:** Can you think of a time when you benefitted from being connected to others? Maybe you were ice skating or swimming or playing tug-of-war.

✳ **THE WEEDS.** Climbers get tired of being roped together. What if you got roped together with someone who talked constantly and drove you crazy? What if they were lazy and you ended up pulling their weight? There would be lots of temptations to disconnect.

You might convince yourself that going it alone is not dangerous. The ground up ahead looks solid, and you're sure nothing terrible will happen. You'll be extra careful. Or you might convince yourself that you're quick enough to catch yourself if you do fall.

As Christians, we disconnect with other believers for similar reasons. We convince ourselves that nothing bad will happen or that we're strong enough to deal with whatever comes our way. Maybe our relationship with our mom and dad hasn't been that great lately, or maybe our Christian friends seem a little boring so we start to disconnect. We decide not to talk to Mom about the hurtful comment our friend made. We choose not to share the information we learned at the sleepover. "It'll all work out," we tell ourselves.

GIRLS: In what situations do you most want to unhook from your mom?

MOMS: Do you remember a time when being linked to godly people helped you? Is there a time when being disconnected hurt you?

Read Proverbs 13:20.

Walking with the wise will bring wisdom. So how can we make sure we continue doing it?

As moms and daughters, keep talking. Set aside time every so often to sit down and talk about whatever is going on. Look up Scriptures, encourage each other, confess sin, and admit weaknesses. Hopefully, our walks have paved the way for continuing to do this.

BOTH: Take a few minutes to write down five more conversations you could have together or "walks" you could take.

THE HILL. Stay linked to Jesus, the guide who knows exactly which route is best for us. He knows how to get us through the slippery spots and craggy cliffs of this life and into the glory of the next.

Jesus isn't someone we need in order to be forgiven and then leave behind. We need his Spirit, his grace, his power, and his love to fill us and guide us every step of the way.

Even after all these conversations, we're still weak and we will still fail. There is not one chapter where I can say, "Well at least I've got that one down. I think I'm doing everything right." I make mistakes; I choose sin; I get stuck in selfishness; I make the wrong choices; but Jesus has forgiven me and his Spirit gives me grace to keep going. He will do the same for you. As we finish our time and you hike off into the future, remember that you can't do it alone. Stay connected to Mom; and most importantly, stay connected to Jesus. What a joy to reach the summit together.

 THE FIELD

- **How can you make sure that you stay connected to each other? To your church? To godly friendships?**
- **Girls, how can you stay close to your dad and glean from his wisdom?**
- **How can you make sure you stay linked in with Jesus?**
- **Take time to pray together about your future journey.**

Appendix
Our Protection

....

NOTE TO MOMS: It's probably been a while since you read "A Word to Moms" found in the beginning of this book, so I will remind you of the purpose of this appendix, which deals with the sensitive but important topic of sexual abuse. Although the topic can feel difficult to broach, the conversation guide below should make it much easier. This appendix is separate from the other talks because it has a slightly different format and because it relates to several of the other chapters—not because it is less significant. Please use this tool after whatever chapter you decide is best, but don't miss the opportunity to have this vital conversation.

....

My husband has an identical twin, and you can imagine the fun they had with that when they were young! Once in sixth grade, he and his brother switched classes in school. All their friends knew it but they kept it secret from their teachers. They pulled off their trick for quite a while as their classmates smothered giggles, until one of the teachers began to suspect the trick. The teacher walked to the other classroom, pointed to the other twin, and yelled, "Imposter!" The class erupted in laughter and the boys high-fived and returned to their rooms.

Secrets can be fun, like the class-switching trick or a plan to surprise your dad with a triple-decker cake you made for his birthday.

GIRLS: What is one of the most fun secrets or surprises you remember?

MOMS: How about you?

Secrets can be used to bring happiness to others, but some secrets can be harmful. Secrets about our bodies usually fall into the second category.

Your body has been created perfectly by God and each part is special, but some parts—the parts that your swimsuit covers—are meant to be private. That means that no one should be touching or asking to look at these parts except for a doctor or a parent who is caring for you. And no one should want you to touch or look at their private parts either. If this has happened to you, it's important that you understand that it's not your fault, and it's just as important that you tell your mom or another trusted adult right away.

GIRLS: Has anyone besides a doctor or parent who is caring for you ever touched your private parts or asked to see them? Has anyone shown you their private parts or asked you to touch them?

Now this whole topic might seem obvious to you. *Of course I know this stuff,* you think to yourself. But sometimes situations happen gradually and they aren't always clear. Someone might touch your shoulder or your knee in a way that seems too familiar. Someone might rub your leg in a way that feels odd and uncomfortable. Or a friend's parent might goof around in the shower during a sleepover and it doesn't feel right to you, but you feel too embarrassed to tell your parents. If you feel too embarrassed, that probably means you should say something. Trust your instincts. Remember, if someone touches you in a way that makes you feel uncomfortable, it's not your fault. If something feels uncomfortable to you, tell Mom or some other trusted adult, even if the person involved is a church member, or a relative, or someone in authority.

MOMS: What kind of touching would make you feel uncomfortable? Describe a touch that would be appropriate from one of your adult friends, and one that would be inappropriate.

GIRLS: What kinds of things have made you feel uncomfortable? (Maybe someone has taken their clothes off or has shown you a movie you don't think you should have seen.) Is there a certain place where you don't like to spend time because of what happens there? Is there any adult or child in your life who makes you feel uneasy?

We talked earlier about how some secrets are fun and some are harmful. If someone asks or forces you to participate in an inappropriate activity, they might then tell you to keep it a secret. That's a harmful secret. Don't keep that secret for a million dollars; in fact, do the opposite. Tell someone you trust immediately. Secrets should be reserved for bringing happiness to others, not for hiding information from people who love you.

GIRLS: What if someone said to you, "Don't tell anyone about this because if you do, something bad is going to happen." Would you tell your mom? Why or why not?

Secrets are for people you trust, and if someone you don't trust asks you to keep a secret about something that makes you uncomfortable, you should never feel obligated to do that.

It's wrong for anyone to threaten you in any way, like telling you that something bad will happen if you share a secret. The best thing you can do for yourself, and for the other person, is to tell someone immediately and get the help you both need.

Sometimes situations are clearly wrong, and sometimes they aren't. Maybe you've talked with your mom about a situation and you really don't think anyone did anything wrong, but you can't shake an uneasy feeling when you're in that situation. It's not wrong to say "no" at these times. "No," you'd rather not sit quite that close. "No," you'd rather not see that movie. "No," you'd rather not turn out the lights in the basement for the game you're playing.

If you're feeling nervous right now, you can breathe easy. Talking about these topics doesn't mean they're going to happen. Most of us will never experience a situation like the ones we discussed today, and most people we meet will interact with us in happy, healthy ways. But open conversations like this help keep it that way.

Everyone has a story, but not everyone has their story straight.

This 52-week devotional from Kristen Hatton helps teens and young adults escape the confusion of the selfie culture and embrace the gospel story where God is the hero. *Get Your Story Straight* frees teens to focus on Jesus and reshapes how they think about grace, identity, and mission. Designed for individual devotional use or in a small-group setting, *Get Your Story Straight* will move teens and young adults toward the freedom that comes from living secure in Christ's love.

New Growth Press
www.newgrowthpress.com